Recognition For
"It's Your Money So Take It Personally®"
and Valerie Coleman Morris:

"Valerie and I became colleagues in the financial world more than a dozen years ago, at a time when it was dominated mostly by men. Valerie is a respected colleague in the financial world and someone who cares about making money matters clearer for everyday people."

~Suze Ormon,
Internationally acclaimed personal finance expert

"Rebounding from the recession requires knowledge, tools and financial foresight. Consider Valerie Coleman Morris your trusted guide. Her approach is welcoming, warm and unique. After this read, your relationship with your money will change for the better.

~Bob McTeer,
Fellow at the National Center for Policy Analysis and former President of the Federal Reserve Bank of Dallas

"I am committed to balancing the scales of justice. My former CNN colleague Valerie Morris is dedicated to helping you balance your budget and financial life."

~Nancy Grace,
Legal commentator and host of the Nancy Grace CNN current affairs show

"Valerie Coleman Morris has used her gifts of humor, intellect and everyday common sense to write a remarkable book that is timely and timeless for people re-examining their relationship with money. Whether you are a college student forging a path of independence or a seasoned executive who manages your own assets, this book will challenge your thinking and improve your decision-making about money. Read it again and again—then pass it to others. This is the gift that keeps on giving!"

~Rayona Sharpnack,
Founder & CEO, Institute for Women's Leadership

D1113416

Brandelyn
Health and wealth!
Valerie Coleman Morris

It's Your Money
So Take It Personally®

By

Valerie Coleman Morris

Published by Aspen Business Group

For information please contact:
Valerie Coleman Morris @www.valeriecolemanmorris.com

ISBN #978-0-615-50175-8
Publishing Company
Aspen Business Group
15861 Dorth Circle
Fort Myers, FL 33908
239-482-5159

Library of Congress Cataloging-in-Publication Data

Morris, Valerie Coleman.
It's Your Money So Take It Personally®:
it's your money so take it personally, -/ by Valerie Coleman Morris
1.Finance, Personal. 2. Retirement income--Planning.
3. Investments. I. Title.

Cover photo: Barbara Meier Photography
Contributing editor: W.B. King
Copy editor: Fane Wolfer
Layout and design: Gene Wiseman & Lavasite Productions

Printed in the United States of America

With love to my grandlittles,
Morgan and Savannah.
Be amazing.

Acknowledgments

My maternal grandmother told me, "We have two lives: the one we learn with, and the one we live; the process is often simultaneous."

Sometimes in life when faced with a great task, we tend to wait for a "more convenient season." It was my former senior manager, Ken Jautz, executive vice president of CNN/USA, who told me, "You've got the content in your head already; write it down!" And so I did. Ken Jautz was the best manager I ever had in my career. My special thanks to him for reminding me that I'm a "problem-resolving" kind of person and encouraging me to write a book that would capture my style of having living room conversations about money with everyday people.

Thanks to my longtime friends and sounding boards: Lois Pitter-Bruce, who fortified my spirit, cheered me up, calmed me down and listened endlessly to every concern related to this book; Mary Savoie-Stephens and Claudia Pryor Malis, who kept my spirit on track and reminded me about the value of marketing time until the right time; and Larry Largente, whose thoughtful counsel and friendship have been ever present since my days as a student at San Jose State University in northern California.

My sincere appreciation goes to those colleagues who have supported the book: Aileen Hernandez, David J. Teece, Suze Ormon, Bob McTeer, Nancy Grace, Congresswoman Jackie Speier, Rayona Sharpnack, Earl G. Graves, Sr., Judge Glenda Hatchett, Nell Merlino, former California State Senator John Vasconcellos, Congresswoman Barbara Lee, Edward Tanenbaum, Dr. Lois Frankel, Helena Brantley, Brad Bunnin and Greg McBride.

Thanks to friends and colleagues for affirming that "You can't pay back love; you can only pass the kindness on to somebody else." These include Virginia Morris, Mary Beth Franklin, Evonne Yancey, Gwendolyn Sykes, Alana Ross, Dr. Brenda Wade, Leigh Teece, Stephanie Elam, Bonnie Price, Dawn Fotopulos, Paula Harrell, and Kim Bardakian. You all provided support at moments when I needed deposits into my emotional bank account.

Thanks to my editor, W.B. (Brad) King, whom I dubbed my Writing Sherpa, for keeping me moving forward and focused in the midst of a process not familiar to me and whose immediate responses to all my questions were always informative and reassuring. Compliments to my copy editor, Fane Wolfer, for his command of grammatical protocols and for taking control when editing with Word's Track Changes got the best of me. Gratitude to Carol Florsheim, who graciously offered her critical eye for detail, provided moment-to-moment answers to my daily, multiple e-mails and phone calls, and responded to my thank-you's with one word: Sisterhood! Special thanks to my personal assistant, Faryn Davis, whose enthusiasm and dedication for this project were priceless. Sincere appreciation to my graphic design group at Lavasite Productions and especially to my publisher, Bill Dueease of Aspen Business Group, for his assistance, reassurances and ever-present humor in the midst of my many challenges while getting this book done.

What comes out of the heart determines the course of your life. I will always especially remember Marcy Hyman, who, in a time of need long ago, was the financial wind beneath my feet. I love and thank my family: my husband, Robert, who has shown me by example the importance of being resilient; my daughters, Michon and Ciara; my son-in-law, James Harris; my grandlittles, Morgan and Savannah; my parents, Bill and Vicki Dickerson; and finally, my maternal grandmother, Janice Logan Baxter, aka "Mudd."

Preface

Bad things happen to well-intentioned people and their money. I'm living proof. I paid a huge price – financially and emotionally–publishing this book. The experience and circumstances in which I found myself were everything *but* business as usual.

It's Your Money So Take It Personally® was scheduled to be released the third quarter of 2010, but publication was held off by delay after delay. The first publishing company I partnered with failed to meet our contractual agreement, leaving this book in a literary limbo. In the middle of the recession, there I was, like so many other people, trying to do the right thing when the rules of the game were changed without notice. Despite my best attempts, I found myself in an unwanted and unexpected situation.

It's Your Money So Take It Personally

I pass along to you what I learned: When bad things happen, step back and focus not on what's *out of your control* but rather on *what you can control.* This rule applies both to your money and to the unfortunate circumstances resulting from the Great Recession that began in December 2007 and continues to impact our national economy.

Many people are still out of work, upside down on their mortgage, and uncertain about their financial future and their ability to stabilize it. The rebound certain economists speak of hasn't felt like a recovery to most Americans, who, despite their best efforts, have not experienced a positive change in their financial standing.

It's Your Money So Take It Personally® provides money-management tools that let you approach your finances in a personalized way. The aim is to "right size" your thinking about what you can control when it comes to your money. As you rebuild after the Great Recession, this book will demonstrate why "getting back to normal" when it comes to money *isn't* wise. Rather, it will help you establish a new normal.

Passing the buck stops here. Learning and committing to understanding what's best for our money's well-being starts now! I offer what I know, what I've personally experienced, and what I've learned about creating, re-creating and maintaining the 21st century form of emancipation: financial freedom.

The key for me was to get smarter. My learning curve from working as a television news anchor to working as a business correspondent happened in real time on CNN in front of nearly 300 million households and businesses. Every night I did my homework and prepared for number-crunching interviews with renowned money specialists. I needed to ask the right questions because they had the answers.

One only has to look to yet another increase in our national debt ceiling to understand that, like many American households, our country too remains troubled. The markets have been volatile. The unemployment rate remains high and the economy has not fully recovered.

My good friend and internationally known economist David J. Teece says in the afterword to this book: "An economy that has investment is an economy that will grow and generate jobs. Individual financial prudence begets societal and governmental prudence. Unfortunately, the reverse is also true, as we have been witnessing for quite some time now. So putting mind over money matters not just for the individual. It matters for families, communities and for our nation."

Thank you for taking this journey with me. Let's step back and focus on how you can control your money, not on how your money is controlling you. This is an opportunity to acquire new skills that will help build confidence in your ability to solve money-management shortfalls. ~Valerie

Valerie Coleman Morris

It's Your Money So Take It Personally

Contents

Valerie Coleman Morris

It's Your Money So Take It Personally

Foreword

Aileen Hernandez

*Founder and Former President,
National Organization for Women (NOW)*

I understand why some people view economics as a "dismal" science. In nearly my ninth decade of life, I'm still learning about money management's best practices thanks to a friend, many years younger than me, who keeps referring to me as her mentor. Valerie Coleman Morris is an Emmy award—winning journalist and financial literacy expert who has written an important book on what people need to know and do about their financial health.

I met Valerie in the very early days of what is now

called the Women's Movement but at that time was more often denigrated as "those women libbers." It was the late 1960s. As a founder of the National Organization for Women, and later elected as its second national president, I got a lot of press in those days. Activist black women, longtime supporters of the civil rights movement in the San Francisco Bay Area, came to me for advice. One group of politically active women decided to form Black Women Organized for Political Action (BWOPA).

However, some BWOPA members (mostly from San Francisco) disagreed about the narrow definition of women's role in society and, in 1973, formed Black Women Organized for Action (BWOA). They announced that "black women must go beyond the traditional fund-raising and into the full gamut of activities that make up the political process, which affects our lives in so many ways." They were off and running, learning new skills and challenging inequities.

Coalescing with other women's rights groups, BWOA founded a credit union for women, elected six women to San Francisco's 11-member Board of Supervisors in 1980 and seated the first black woman as president of the board (for receiving the majority of votes in the election). All of this made news and media executives slowly added young black women journalists (among them Valerie) to their staffs. Other barriers began to fall, and the TV image of multiracial San Francisco began to come closer to reflecting its actual population.

While BWOA was about the power, the glory and the responsibility of leadership, it was also about teaching money management – motivating the members to get new skills, raise their expectations about personal success and encourage their children to do the same.

Valerie was as innovative then as she is now and expanded her career ambitions. She drew from her journalistic pursuits and her personal life as a wife and mother to contribute to the financial needs of her family. Her television news reports and community affairs programs spoke to all genders and races and became more oriented toward the rapidly changing lives of those in the baby-boom generation. And when her marriage ended in divorce, she was faced with the unpleasant reality that, when it came to financial security, she was on her own.

She didn't go to pieces. She concentrated on her strengths and fearlessly began to build a new life for herself and her children. As a talented communicator, she took to the airwaves and shared what she was learning with a ready-made audience of women, men and children – each struggling to understand money-management practices. Beyond the basics, Valerie also discussed the tough issues, such as how gender equality would affect the division of merged financial resources. Who gets what and why?

Her book embodies the counter-philosophy that emerged from Valerie's life experiences. She was to rely on herself for financial security and pay it forward while anticipating her long-range financial needs. It was not easy, but by the time she had paid off the last of her marriage-accumulated debt, she had a new set of marketable skills that gave her new career options.

What makes this book valuable is that Valerie Coleman Morris has managed to capture what is actually happening in the lives of everyday, real people. She not only shares her experiences, she adds what she has learned from interactions with thousands of people over the years through forums, panels and face-to-face discussions. Valerie Coleman Morris has credibility with a diverse audience. This book is full of practical information for improving our personal relationship with that often elusive promise of lifelong financial security.

Valerie Coleman Morris

It's Your Money So Take It Personally

Chapter 1

It's Never Too Late and It's Never Too Early

"Life is a succession of lessons which must be lived to be understood." — Helen Keller

Most people didn't see it coming. It happened in everyone's backyard. The economic meltdown that has defined the past four-plus years left financial disarray everywhere. No one was immune. Countless jobs were lost, retirement accounts dwindled, loans defaulted, home values plummeted, and foreclosure and unemployment rates skyrocketed. But had the average American been better equipped with the

1

necessary mental and emotional financial disciplines and tools, there might have been fewer casualties.

Our new, post-recession economy will require people of all ages to be lifelong learners of money matters and, most importantly, our country's system of commerce and finance called capitalism. That's why, whether in good economic times or bad, managing your finances requires diligence and consistent oversight.

Definition of Capitalism:

Individuals and companies are allowed to compete for their own economic gain. By and large, free-market forces determine the prices of goods and services.

In order to survive and succeed in the 21st century, it is imperative for anyone facing economic hardship or seeking better money-management strategies to understand and use our capitalistic system to his or her benefit. There are lots of tools at your disposal. I'll provide insights on how to better utilize them. All I ask of you is to assess your financial habits honestly and embrace my recipe for fiscal liberation, one step at a time. I believe strongly that every person has immense capacity to redirect his or her respective financial course.

As these pages unfold, I will provide practical, logical suggestions for how you can improve your relationship with money. As English philosopher Francis Bacon famously said, "Knowledge is power." By reading this book, you will gain the power to positively change your financial outlook.

For the past 40 years, I have been in the field of broadcasting, and for nearly half of that I have concentrated on financial literacy. My last on-air post was as one of CNN's business anchors for its various domestic and international networks. As a result, I've been afforded many wonderful opportunities to learn and grow from interactions with financial experts, business leaders, policymakers, entrepreneurs and countless hard-working Americans.

Since then, I have concentrated my efforts toward working with people of all ages – from children to the elderly – concerning money issues. I have been able to address this multi-generational demographic through a radio program I created called "With the Family in Mind," which has aired three times a week on CBS Network Radio for nearly 30 years. The radio program's goal is to promote a dialogue about how different generations and genders approach money management, and it was the foundation for this book.

Silver Lining

Although the National Bureau of Economic Research – the independent group of economists charged with determining when economic downturns start and finish – says the recession began to ease in the summer of 2009, it remains difficult for many hard-working men and women to make ends meet. Many economists say the worst of it may be over, but the financial winds of change continue to blow. It has been said that you can't change the direction of the wind; you can only reset your sails to reach your destination. The destination to which I want to direct you is your financial independence.

Is it possible that this recession had a silver lining? Absolutely! Reassessing and improving your relationship with your money has never been easier because so many people have never been so motivated. These days, learning about money is considered the smart thing to do, and personal finance is the new hot topic at the water cooler.

Money decisions always have consequences. But this recession, which officially began in December 2007, captured everybody's attention. Many lost a home to escalating mortgage rates, lost their job or are now in their twilight years without a retirement plan. These sobering realities have families proactively

4

communicating about money. Cooperative economic practices, such as family budgeting and planning all aspects of a sound financial future, should be being discussed at kitchen tables from San Francisco to Boston. But, all too often, the conversation never begins.

The current economic crisis and the repercussions of raising the debt ceiling will be with us for years to come. To achieve a full financial recovery, every person must gain the knowledge needed to support smart money management, which requires that you recognize poor financial habits and learn the long-term value of compounding. You must compound not just dollars, but the information you've gained in the process. This approach mirrors the message so eloquently stated in the aforementioned inspirational words of Helen Keller: "Life is a succession of lessons which must be lived to be understood."

My paramount concern and what I hope will become your new money mind-set is that you aren't working for your money, but making your money work for you. Regardless of your circumstances, it is time to get back to basics, starting by evaluating your monthly budget and creating a new financial frontier.

The good news is that as we collectively attempt

to emerge from this recession, we have the unique opportunity to evaluate our relationship to money and start anew. People from all walks of life are searching for ways to better sustain the health and wealth of their family, and they're making a concerted effort to change.

If you count yourself among those who believe that they made too many financial mistakes in years past, give yourself permission to change your perspective. You didn't make mistakes. Rather, you experienced a series of *mi$$ed-takes*. They were cumulative, yes, but these past decisions do not have to define your financial well-being moving forward.

Those struggling to gain financial wellness need to know that it will require a different approach. It's essential that we use concrete methods to assist us in recalculating our relationship with money. Perhaps the most important step before you decide what to do with your money is to first understand how you feel about your money.

The rearview-mirror concept

Thanks to my progressive, insightful parents, I've been a world citizen my entire life. I'm a proud Air Force brat, and I loved the many experiences it afforded. I had lived in England, France, Scotland and

Japan by the time I was a junior in high school.

I learned life lessons throughout my travels
as a young girl. My father, William O. "Bill"
Dickerson, a lieutenant colonel in the United States
Air Force, served with the Tuskegee Airmen and
was responsible for ground transportation. This
division comprised dedicated, determined young
men who became America's first black military
-airmen during World War II, at a time when many
Americans wrongly thought that black people lacked
intelligence, skill, courage and patriotism.

It was in 1954 while abroad that I heard my father
speak of the "rearview mirror" for the first time. I
wasn't old enough to understand the reference or to
know that an important lesson was coming my way.
He told me: "If you look in the rearview mirror for
too long, you won't know what you run into." Okay,
I thought, he means it's always best to keep an eye on
the road ahead of you.

But as I grew older I realized the full meaning
of Dad's message: "Remember where you've been,
and understand where you're headed. If you let
old thoughts dominate your thinking, you won't
be able to prepare for the future. If you look in the
rearview mirror too long, you may not recognize an

7

opportunity in front of you." This theory is the core of my foundation.

Val-uable Money Tip:

Financial mi$$ed-takes are advantageous experiences that can positively influence future decisions.

Over the course of my life, I've heard the rearview-mirror reference countless times. Each time I heard or recalled his quote, whether as a frustrated teen or as an overwhelmed single mother, I knew I needed to hear it. Now I, too, convey the concept to my daughters, friends and the many people I have come to know over the course of my life and professional career.

I learned my first profound and lasting money lesson at a very young age. I was 8 years old. I was back in the states in North Philadelphia, happily visiting with cousins. My family managed to make these trips when my father's overseas assignments concluded.

One day I tried to use an English shilling instead of an American quarter to buy a bottle of Coke from a vending machine. My cousins doubled over laughing. Up to that point, my day-to-day money references were in pounds, shillings, francs and military paper currency called "scrip." While I understood the intrinsic value of currency, I wasn't as familiar with these things called dimes, quarters and dollars. When my cousins finally regained their composure, they showed me the difference between the two coins. I drank the cold Coke but also felt chilled by the embarrassment. That day I learned a lesson about the importance of understanding the value of money and my relationship to it. A financial seed was planted. It remains at the root of my personal relationship with money.

I've had my share of hardships and *mi$$ed-takes*. When I was first married, I was the major breadwinner as well as the manager of our family finances, which I handled to the best of my abilities. Then in 1991, while in my early-40s, I became a divorced single mother of two daughters. Reality set in.

Because divorce rates are unfortunately high, I understand that many people reading this book have gone though the trauma and drain of a divorce. It's hard enough to deal with the emotional component – how it impacts your family and children – but you also have to consider the financial implications.

Getting divorced in a community-property state such as California was a discouraging educational experience for me. As I began the process of rebuilding my life, I could have directed my energy in an unproductive manner, such as being vindictive or acting like a victim. Instead I chose to get even – not as in getting back at someone, but rather by focusing on clearing the family debt my ex-husband and I had incurred. It was the only way to improve *my* future money picture. It gave me control. Today, my credit score is my favorite number and it starts with the number 8!

The "B" word and its value

My fundamental approach to money management: You can't spend more money than you earn. That may sound simplistic. But how do you control spending if you don't *know* what you're spending your money on? Rather than grasping at the ghost of your money's past, look into your money's future by using the *B* word: budget. For many, the word *budget* is a scary one. It's associated with being a spendthrift or penny-pincher. So, let's call it a spending plan that allows you to track your spending, saving and investing habits.

While the importance of budgeting will be covered in greater detail in forthcoming chapters, keeping track of every dollar spent sounds tedious and overwhelming. But it doesn't have to be. For example, start by writing down everything you spend for just one month. This includes your $4 morning latte and your $2,000 monthly mortgage payment. It matters less what your income level is; what matters more is what you do with your money and why. To accumulate, grow and preserve your money (however much or little) requires discipline.

A Generational Lens

Ralph Waldo Emerson, an American essayist and philosopher, wrote: "What lies behind us and what lies before us are tiny matters compared to what lies within us." This quote speaks to me because I firmly believe each of us has the ability to change undesirable habits.

Defining a person's character is a subjective, difficult process. Emerson's quote opens the door to the possibility of finding inner strength for change, but for many it will be a long journey. There are touchstones that aid in the pursuit. For example, I count myself among the baby boomers, the generation of approximately 76 million born between 1946 and 1964. While a significant number of us who fall within this demographic are nearing retirement age, a growing number of my peers are faced with the new reality that I call "The Age of Un-Retirement," which I will discuss in Chapter 9.

I am deeply concerned about the issues baby boomers are facing, a generation caught – either by choice or by circumstance – in the middle, sandwiched between the generation that produced us and the generation we produced. Creating, maintaining and facilitating financial independence throughout generations should be every family's business.

As a wife, proud mother and grandmother, I look at financial wellness through a generational lens. My daughters are members of Generation X, those born between 1965 and 1981. Next is Generation Y, or the Echo Generation (1981 to 2000), followed by Generation Z, aka the Millennials. My two grandchildren, whom I affectionately call my "grandlittles," are members of the last. These generations, including the various cultures, ethnicities and philosophies they comprise, will be further discussed. But for the moment, suffice it to say, great differences exist in how each respectively approaches money-management issues. For example, many young people prefer online banking and banking via smart phone, whereas a significant number of older people still lean toward making a personal visit to their local branch. The way in which we handle transactions and investments will change with technology, but our fundamental relationship with our money should remain consistent.

The lessons that are provided here can be used as early as the age of 3. It is imperative to teach children the difference between wants and needs – a money lesson that many adults never learned. As a result, these adults have conditioned themselves to make poor financial choices then suffer the fate of not having saved for education and retirement.

Not unlike a parent introducing a child to music or art in infancy, providing children with a "dollars and *sense*" mind-set as early as preschool will make them aware about money and its value. It is never too early to *bank* on a child's future by jump-starting his or her approach to money matters.

As we age, it is imperative to figure out the things that trigger our money-making decisions. They can be deep-seated or dwell just below the surface. The way in which people deal with money provides a portal into the way they handle the complexities of life. Dr. Brenda Wade, a colleague and friend, is a nationally renowned psychologist best known for her dynamic, love-centered approach to personal transformation. She recently wrote: "What an opportunity to think through and bring new resolve to fulfilling our life goals. Writing goals, not resolutions, actually works. [When] properly constructed, goals constitute a blueprint, a plan, and planning really works."

Regardless of age, financial goals are not overwhelming when they include incremental, deliberate acts of money management. If you were to accomplish one proactive, progressive step each month, at the end of the year you would have 12 financial goals satisfied (see Chapter 11 for the **Val-uable Monthly Calendar** to-do list).

The goals can be small. For example, a doable and important goal is committing to automatic monthly deposits into savings and retirement accounts. Again, the idea is to approach redefining your economic landscape incrementally. Determining how best to approach goals regardless of your generation will be covered in specific detail in forthcoming chapters. It's never too late and never too early to get a grip on your financial future.

Val-uable Money Mantra:

If you find a dollar, do you ask, "What can I do with this dollar?" or "What can this dollar do for me?" A person with a wealth-building mind-set will embrace the latter because he or she understands the power of investing in one's future.

A Professional Approach

I'm often on the road engaging inquisitive audiences of all ages on the subject of financial literacy. When I speak to people about how *and why* they spend their money, I often reference one of my favorite games: golf.

Hitting balls at the practice range and repeating drills result in an enhanced skill set. Dedicated golfers are then able to shave strokes from their game and get closer to achieving par. Similarly, you can improve your "money game" by understanding indicators such as credit scores, credit card annual percentage rates, insurance premiums, investment earnings and countless other money metrics. Practicing financial oversight will better prepare you to appropriately and consistently save money.

My maternal grandmother, Janice Logan Baxter, would often say to me, "The elevator to success is broken; you have to take the steps." When it comes to successful money management, too many people continually ride elevators that drop them off on the wrong floor or stall between floors without good reason. Instead they should take the steps toward financial solvency.

It's Your Money So Take It Personally

Chapter 2

—ᴍ—

Back to Basics:
Val-uable Money Tips

"I do not try to dance better than anyone else. I only try to dance better than myself." — Mikhail Baryshnikov

I recently presented a seminar in California on the best practices in personal finance. I began by telling the crowd simply: You can't spend more than you make. Laughter filled the room. Their faces conveyed a collective thought: Duh.

Then I said it a second time. The nervous laughter in the room began to dissipate, and I sensed that members of the audience were beginning to internally acknowledge some of their own financial shortcomings. After I made the statement a third time, I noticed that I had caught their attention and they were ready to listen and learn the importance of this simple fact. Why? Because they knew that "you can't spend more than you make" was correct. This basic money concept isn't rocket science, but it represents reality. In order to grab hold of your finances, have a sustainable recovery from the recession and begin living in your "new normal" money mind-set, you have to get back to the basics.

According to the U.S. Census Bureau, the average 25-year-old American makes approximately $32,000 per year. The median household annual income is $50,221. The average American family annually overspends their income by 20 percent. This is a serious problem and underscores the need for an accounting of inflow (income) and outflow (expenses). It's known as a budget.

The "B" word continued

So how do you assign or pick a set dollar amount to be your monthly budget? A quick way is to determine your total household income. Next, choose an amount (a "spending budget") that is lower than your total household income. Divide that number by

12. The new number is your monthly budget. This quick calculation gives you a logical, workable dollar amount that you can wrap your brain around quickly. The money "saved" – the difference between your actual income and your expenses – can be put toward retirement (see Chapter 11 for examples) or other necessary and determined goals. Every member of the family can and should participate in this multiple-generation exercise so that everyone becomes familiar with the idea of what can (budgeted items) and what can't (what's not budgeted) be spent.

Raising money smart children

We teach our children that reading is fundamental. We need to teach them that learning about money is *fun* and *mental*. Money involves mathematics, which is another critical skill. When my grandson Morgan was in second grade, I taught him how to multiply numbers by 9 without the aid of a calculator or computer by using just his hands. First, hold up ten fingers in front of you. When multiplying 9 times 3, simply drop the third finger on your right hand. How many fingers (on both hands) are to the right of your third finger? Two. How many fingers are to the left of the third finger? Seven. Put them together and you have 27, which is the answer to 9 times 3.

Making numbers and money management *fun*

and *mental* increases financial cooperation from your children and your ability to budget within your means. Though you may not readily see the value of this little exercise, it is but one of many opportunities to engage and entertain while educating. The reference point is that, since all numbers represent a value, understanding numbers will help children begin to assign value to money as their critical mathematics skills grow.

My grandmother used to say, "If there isn't a piece of the pie left for you, make another pie." Consider this book a recipe for your financial pie. Keeping in mind that every pie is different because of varying circumstances or ingredients, you can create your pie by dissecting your financial portfolio and then reconstructing it with the information I will provide. My grandmother's message is mine: Don't wait around for someone to provide for you. We need to be accountable for ourselves.

Val-uable Money Mantra:
It's your money so take it personally®.

It's not so much what your income level is; what matters most is what you do with your money and why. The same basic disciplines are required. I encourage you to employ a consistent, deliberate and systematic approach to establish and maintain your financial well-being. Keep in mind that this is not a destination-based mission; rather, this is an ongoing journey. You should view your money as a living entity that can change your life for the better or for the worse. My objective is to focus on the former and place you on the path to financial independence.

The best way to approach financial wellness is to get yourself in the right frame of mind. This is a long-term learning model. And when you are in the right frame of mind, the payoff is self-reliance. What better gift could you give yourself?

Treat Money Like Oxygen

In order to survive we need to breathe. I have a postcard in my office with a quote from Buddha: "Things to do today: Exhale, inhale, exhale. *Ahhhh.*" I reference this quotation often because money, like oxygen, is our common denominator —— without it, you can't survive. Think of money as if it were your oxygen.

<hr>

Val-uable Money Mantra:
Treat your money like oxygen.
Breathe life into your portfolio.

<hr>

At some point, or at various junctures, your

relationship to money will cause anxiety. Anxiety is part of human nature. In times of financial stress or worry, remember to practice breathing deeply, as it will help you relieve anxiety and focus on the money matter at hand. Physiologically, this exercise is similar to the Lamaze approach to birthing.

Here's how I do it. When I'm feeling anxious, my head sinks into my shoulders, which tighten and push upward toward my ears. During these moments, I take a succession of deep, measured breaths, inhaling through my nose and exhaling through my mouth. I exhale slowly, as if I were blowing all the air out of a balloon. My shoulders ease and slowly drop. My mind becomes freer, allowing for clearer decision-making. Shallow, quick breathing never results in good decisions. When we breathe, we allow ourselves to feel more relaxed so that we can address the real problem, not the stress.

In my seminars, while speaking with people about money matters, I have sensed great stress. Being what some people call a "toucher," I have often reached out to someone in distress by touching their arm, or even grasping their hand. This lets them know physically that we have the ability to connect and discuss and take the first steps toward resolving their situation. People leave these encounters realizing that they *can* take control of their financial future *if* they incorporate simple exercises – such as remembering to breathe, which helps us think clearly. This approach won't alleviate unfortunate or challenging circumstances, but it allows for the possibility of compartmentalizing and tackling respective money dilemmas.

Removing stress from the situation, however difficult, will fortify your confidence. If there is a problem, face it immediately. When you're dealing with creditors chasing you down for payments, for example, don't avoid them. Face them armed with controlled, stress-free breathing and knowledge of your rights and your options.

Pace Wins the Race

With your breathing in place, you're ready to consider your financial education as a marathon, not a sprint. This thought should always be first and foremost on your mind. Identifying *mi$$ed-takes* and learning from them is the goal. I will not offer quick fixes whether your trouble is credit card debt, refinancing home loans or budgeting. The reason is simple: There are no quick fixes. But know that small changes add up to big results.

Correcting your approach to financial wellness should be no different than how a smoker approaches quitting. Many smoke-cessation specialists say it's not a matter of cutting down from a pack of cigarettes a day to five cigarettes a day. The smoker must quit completely, which requires a strong will, supported by a new mind-set. Remember, money management is a marathon and you'll need all your strength (and oxygen) to finish each race and reach each money goal.

Roberta "Bobbi" Gibb, who in 1966 became the first woman to run the Boston Marathon, said after crossing the finish line, "I thought about how many preconceived prejudices would crumble when I trotted right along for 26 miles." Roberta broke down long-standing social barriers. But we all have personal barriers – preconceived notions of ourselves – especially when it comes to money. I've heard excuses such as "I got into debt because I was offered credit cards in college and overspent" or "I simply *can't* save money." *Mi$$ed-takes* might force you into the mind-set that your track record will be forever flawed. This is *not* the case.

For example, let's say you are 50 and you haven't saved a dime for your retirement. Is it too late? The answer is no. Will you have to *drastically* change your spending habits? Absolutely. A 45-year-old who wants to retire with $1 million at age 65 will have to set aside nearly $1700 each month to reach that goal; a 55-year-old would need to save more than $5400 every month for the next ten years. While this isn't easy to do, the point is it *is* doable. With nearly 11,000 baby boomers turning 50 every day – roughly one every 7 minutes – more and more people are realizing that retirement (and the need for retirement income) is rapidly approaching.

Golf and money smarts

Most of us understand the benefits of staying physically active. It keeps me centered so that I can tackle all of the issues in my life, financial or otherwise. Growing up, I didn't play baseball, basketball or soccer. My sport was dance. My mother enrolled me in my first ballet class at the age of 3. I danced – ballet, modern, jazz – for the next 30 years. Dance lessons helped me learn structure, which I applied to all areas of my personal, business and financial life.

Roughly ten years ago I started playing golf. Even with all of its challenges, the game nonetheless provides me with a sense of serenity. Much like finances, there are metrics to golf, including the all-important one: keeping score. I encourage children – especially young girls – to look for a free youth program offered at a public golf course and learn the game's fundamentals. Knowing the basics and being deliberate with your approach to the game can contribute to reshaping your approach to managing your finances.

I equate the game to a mental annuity stream. An annuity is an agreement set up so you receive fixed payments on an investment for a lifetime. Often when it comes to taking the time to learn about managing their money, people (many of them women) say they have no time to learn, that their lives are jammed. Then they ask me, "How can I find a balance between work and family in my life?" I tell them that balance is a soft goal. When has their life ever balanced 50-50 consistently? One day it may be 80-20 in favor of work, and the next day it may be 65-35 in favor of family. Much like the game of golf, having a routine as you approach tasks is important. A routine helps you meet the challenges you face on any given day. That's why I suggest working to "integrate" family life and work life. Who knows what will come with each day? Discipline is the message of your mental annuity stream. It's what keeps you focused on your financial game so that you are better prepared to manage (integrate) life every day rather than trying to balance everything to equal.

Any form of athletic activity contributes to your

becoming physically fit, which in turn will allow you to be financially fit. For example, after a brisk walk or hitting balls at the practice range, I will come home and handle my online-banking tasks (I set aside at least one hour each week). I choose this time because my mind is clear and free. This is as opposed to sitting down after a stressful day and trying to handle money issues, which can feel like trying to do the impossible. Unfortunately, too many people tend to deal with their money in moments of angst. Change that pattern of behavior. You can't time the stock market, but you can time your money-management sessions.

The Tribe Has Spoken

When getting back to basics, often it is helpful to reach far into the annals of history to understand where the concept of money originated. We must also dismiss the myth that money is the root of all evil. (Indeed, Saint Timothy warned that the *love of money* is the root of all kinds of evil. So while despicable Ponzi scheme creators such as Bernard Madoff are evil, money itself is not.)

For many civilizations and tribes throughout the centuries, those who could count were placed in charge of goods and services to disperse among the tribe or trade with other tribes. Bartering, which was the first method of exchange, originated in Sumer, a region known as the Cradle of Civilization located in southern Mesopotamia, in modern-day Iraq. This was the birthplace of writing, the wheel, agriculture, the arch and the plow.

The Laws of Eshnunna (circa 1930 BC) helped to formalize the role of money in civil society, including amounts of interest on debt, fines for wrongdoing and compensation for various infractions of formalized law. We've come a long way since the shekel, which was Sumer's first unit of weight and currency. Over the years our method of exchanging goods and services morphed into capitalism, which was instituted around the 16th century in Europe, although its roots date back to the time of the Shekel. We need to instill in the next generation the benefits of capitalism. It's not a dirty word! It is essentially a system in which neighbors create goods and services and assign such things a monetary value.

We are individually instrumental in the continuation of this economic model. We each play our part working to create goods and services and using respective payment for those services to buy other goods and services. Capitalism is a tremendous cycle of events that can be beneficial to a number of individuals when due diligence is applied. We are all members of this economic tribe. How we handle our money impacts us not only on an individual level but as a country, and further as an integral part of the global economy.

Understanding Val-uable Mantra

I consider something to be doable when I can assign a simple reminder to myself, a mantra that becomes part of my everyday processes. For example, my wallet is very tidy because I believe the way you keep your money is the way you spend your money.

Mantras are another way of instilling a habit. My grandson Morgan, for example, will say "I really need" or "I really want." Even at 9 years old, he catches himself and says, "Is this one of those want things or need things?" He is being taught these important money concepts so he'll know to ask the right questions when experiencing the exchange of goods and services in a store or with money saved in his piggy bank. Right now it may be bubble gum (for bubble-blowing competitions with his aunt "Tia," my eldest daughter, Michon) or small toys he stashes in his school backpack, but one day it will be a car or a house. Instilling money mantras at a young age will allow and build appreciation for making informed decisions as the child grows into an adult.

Older people, too, need a money mantra. My dad, who passed away nearly ten years ago, knew about ATMs and online banking but preferred going to the bank and giving his money to "his" teller. If she wasn't there, then he would come back the following day. As a retired man he had the time to do it, but the other, more important aspect of this behavior was that it was an emotional decision. His generation, those who lived through the Great Depression, have a tangible intimacy with their money, whereas a member of Generation X or Generation Y–perhaps my father's teller–is more comfortable with online banking and credit purchases.

I was a busy young mother, and now I'm a busy grandmother. Like many baby boomers, I juggle a hectic schedule, and if I can simplify or speed up anything in my routine, such as banking, shopping or running errands, I will. My pattern used to be, whenever possible, to consolidate money with one financial institution in order to expedite access to my accounts. Now, I shop rates and best customer-service practices with a vengeance. These days I want more diversity when it comes to finding the right financial institution for my needs. My longtime loyalty to my bank was good for the bank but not always for me. I looked outside traditional banking and incorporated credit unions into my choices of financial services. While both offer similar services, banks are for-profit business corporations owned by private investors; credit unions are nonprofit financial cooperatives owned by members.

I utilize online banking and visit the ATM regularly but not randomly. My dad would often ask, "Are you going to get money out of the wall again?" And I would give him a knowing smile. Soon it became a ritual; whenever he passed an ATM, he would say, "That's where Valerie wants me to get my money – out of the wall."

Reiteration, or developing personal mantras, is an easy way in which we can train ourselves to learn what our mind, spirit and heart really want. Mantras provide clarity. The majority of financial decisions unfortunately are made when you are not thinking clearly. That's why your mantras should be considered prophylactics against *unprotected spending*, a term I use to describe spending habits that we do without any forethought or planning. Not unlike unprotected sex, *unprotected spending* is a risky, impetuous act with potentially serious, long-lasting consequences.

Some people are happy to buy clothes off the

rack, including all the accessories; others prefer to have their clothes designed and tailored specifically to their taste. When it comes to financial planning, however, I think that most people, given a choice, want ready-made financial advice that is just handed to them. Letting someone else decide feels easier. But, much like with clothing, one size generally doesn't fit all when it comes to money management. Each of us has our own respective strengths and weakness in this area. I encourage everyone to have money talks and ask money questions of all generations within their family unit. In doing so, be sure to listen for new money mantras and mind-sets and to improve and reinforce existing ones.

A great American tradition is family-owned and -operated businesses. The reason the majority of family-owned businesses do not survive beyond the third generation is because the elders don't have a succession plan in place. Understandably, many want to stay in business as long as they are healthy and well. But their children – the potential future owners of the business – might have a different approach that needs to be expressed, validated and incorporated. The lack of communication creates a divide that causes failure rates to increase.

In the same respect, when it comes to family

money, however large or small, if you want to have a sustainable legacy of wealth, the tribal leader of the family should be sure that the best bean counter is on the job.

In most households, women, who do not necessarily make the most money within the family structure, are the family money managers.

As I watch the next generation of young women – girls from 8 to 12 years old, otherwise known as the "tweens" – evolve, I want to empower them and their parents by providing a money mind-set that keeps them from becoming the next generation of debtors.

Another area of change with respect to money management within the family: Roles are no longer gender-defined. I believe the diversity of money-management roles indicates a more nurturing environment that takes better advantage of family members' strengths.

Family money responsibilities should be handled by the adult who is the most deliberate and consistent regarding managing family money needs. While money decisions among heads of households should be made in a collaborative way, the responsibility for executing transparent and on-time management of family finances should rest with the adult who is determined to be the family's chief financial officer (CFO).

Lottery Winners Aren't Always Lucky

Growing wealth and attaining wealth quickly are two different concepts. Most people will focus their approach to money management on the former, absent a windfall. Recently, I came across one of my favorite Warren Buffet quotes: "Price is what you pay. Value is what you get."

After reading this quote I was brought back to my days working as a news anchor at Channel 2 in Los Angeles. I was assigned a story on the California State Lottery. A group had formed called "Lottery Winners Anonymous." These were men and women who had won multiple millions but were continually bankrupt until the next annuitized payment cycle. The lesson is that you can give people a lot of money, but without being taught discipline and restraint they could blow it. A similar situation exists for young athletes and entertainers. The reality is, just because you've earned a lot of money doesn't mean you know how to manage it.

This particular news segment began with me awaiting an approaching helicopter. Inside was a "millionaire" taking flying lessons. However, in order for him to fly to the interview, he had to borrow funds from his family because he spent the first installment of winnings in less than six months. Cars were bought, fancy 12-person trips to Aspen were taken and the list went on.

The lottery spokesperson I interviewed said that countless winners make the same *mi$$ed-takes* over and over again with unexpected money windfalls. Many people are making similar *mi$$ed-takes* with *hard-earned* money.

How hard is winning the lottery? Imagine a two-story, four-bedroom house filled floor to ceiling with golf balls. One is marked red and you have to find it blindfolded. In New York, for example, the chance of winning the grand prize lottery drawing is approximately one in 45 million. Every now and then when the lottery reaches an astronomical number, I will put down a few dollars and take my chances. But there are people that will take funds from savings to play the lottery or gamble.

Apply the failed logic of gambling to Buffet's quote: "Price is what you pay. Value is what you get." Buffet, who has made his name and fortune by profitably investing in troubled companies, recently invested $5 billion in Bank of America. His move suggests the banking sector is a safer investment now than it was in 2008 and underscores that money management requires due diligence, patience and foresight. Do not underestimate your value. Understand your assets and limitations.

What's Your Bottom Line?

Before a person can approach the concept of investing, they have to know that they have money they can afford to invest. There are any number of reasons the average person does not invest his or her money, but among the top excuses is, "I don't have enough money to invest." The only way a person can know whether they have additional money to invest is if they have a detailed account of their monthly bills and discretionary spending. You will know what your discretionary spending is if you have created a budget that identifies how much money you make and how much mandatory monthly expenses you have. What remains when you subtract your mandatory monthly expenses from your income is discretionary and is often used for entertainment, shopping or other purchases. That amount or a portion of it could be redirected to an investment. No matter the amount you set aside, a sound financial plan will allow for small to large investments that will make your money work for you. Before investing, be sure you have saved enough to cover at least three to six months' worth of living expenses, you have health insurance and you have an identified goal for which the invested money will be used (a house, a car, education, retirement and so forth).

In your 20s: Saving for Retirement

When I speak to 20-somethings, I implore them to understand that the single most important thing they can do is start saving for their retirement. They invariably say, "How can I save money? I'm barely getting by." My stock response: "It is not a matter of *how much* you save. It could be $5 or $250 a month. It is a matter of developing the mind-set of systematic, consistent saving." I also encourage building an emergency fund. The frame of mind should be that the retirement account is money being saved for your distant future needs. The emergency fund is being saved for unexpected events and isn't touched unless a catastrophic emergency occurs. This younger generation, and how they should approach money management, will be covered in greater detail in Chapter 6.

Getting back to basics comes down to changing your concept of how you want your money to work for you. This is your bottom line. I will not advise a person with limited knowledge of their finances and the stock market to invest. These individuals rightly do not have the confidence because they are not educated on the process. You might not know these fundamentals yet; this book will provide you the tools for exploration. But like my grandmother said, you need to make your own pie – then consume it one sliver at a time.

Education Provides Insight

I believe in education by any means necessary. Not unlike setting aside one hour per week to conduct online banking and deal with money-related needs. I have a few recommendations when beginning a journey to become more financially literate. Read the "What's News" column of *The Wall Street Journal* as well as the first paragraph of articles in the "Front Section". What this will do is allow you to become familiar with the world of finance incrementally. If investing is a far-off goal and you are simply trying to make ends meet, focus on balancing your monthly finances and reference your credit union or banking institution's website, which offers resources on money-management techniques. These are the baby steps. It is that easy.

Val-uable Money Mantra:
Be proactive and participate.
Tiny money-management adjustments add up!

There are books that I continually turn to for inspiration and dependable, clear, straightforward knowledge, including *Welcome to Your Financial Life* by prolific financial writer Virginia Morris. One of life's charming coincidences: Virginia is a colleague and a friend, and while we share the same initials and last name, we are not related. When giving gifts to those in their 20s and 30s, I often include that financial guide along with a check. In the subject line of the check I write, "The first deposit for your retirement fund." From among my mantras I add this note to the gift card: "The best time to start saving for your retirement is in your 20s and 30s. This allows your money to grow untouched over the years and reap the benefit of the magic of compounding, which in simple terms is interest earned on top of interest. Here's to your health and wealth."

Val-uable Money Tip:
The best time to start saving for your retirement is in your 20s and 30s.

Financial education has to be ongoing, and there are various resources to turn to whether it's a book, television or the Web. As in most cases, education is best delivered when it is entertaining or grabs your attention. The recession, as a result of being atop the headlines, got everyone's interest and made them pay closer attention to their personal money. When we look back with historical hindsight, we will find that this period will be considered a progressive, proactive time for the average American and their relationship to their money.

As noted in Chapter 1, my initial financial education came at a severe price. My divorce was my wake-up call. I immediately knew I had to play catch-up on multiple fronts. I had to acquire the money knowledge necessary to dissolve the marriage, figure out the financially related decisions I should make to pick up the pieces of my formerly coupled life, and decide how best to move forward.

As a baby boomer, I was among the first generation of full-time working women. We married and believed "what's yours is mine, and what's mine is yours." It didn't matter who was contributing the bulk of the money to the household. My primary concern was taking care of my children's education, and I didn't fully consider my retirement years. And why should I have? No one told me otherwise; no one talked to the women of my generation about the importance of saving for retirement or about what money wisdom would be needed should we be faced with an uncoupled future. We weren't provided with money-management rules or advice. It was learn as you go, and many of us made mistakes – or, as I prefer to call them, *mi$$ed-takes*. Today you have the benefit of readily available information and resources to acquire the knowledge needed to make better-informed decisions about your financial future. My generation didn't. This is the reason why I am so committed to sharing my experiences with you.

Personal money management is not a competition. It doesn't matter where you have been or what you have done in relation to your finances. Like Mikhail Baryshnikov said, "I only try to dance better than myself." This book's message is the consistent reminder that *it's your money so take it personally*®.

Deep breaths…center yourself…let's move forward.

Chapter 3

$aving Your Assets

"Courage consists in the power of self-recovery."
— Ralph Waldo Emerson

People are more willing to talk about sex than about money. If you ask a person how much money they make a year, they'll look at you as if you've morphed into an alien creature. While it's not polite to ask such pointed questions in mixed company, what about within a family unit? The most important step in attaining financial independence is having the willingness to speak openly about money and assets with the people closest to you: your spouse or partner, children, parents, siblings, and other close relatives. This dialogue will help you to determine the money matters and manners that are at work in your family, for better or for worse. Clarity about your relatives' money habits and money disciplines (or lack thereof) is necessary to help keep your own financial house in order and in focus.

In many families, discussing money is forbidden–and in many cultures it is considered taboo. This is why adopting a progressive, transparent approach to money management can represent a priceless change in thinking for multiple generations. It's a fact: When money is not discussed in families, it leads to systemic problems, such as late bill payments, decreasing credit scores and not saving for education and retirement. This is one dilemma all generations have in common.

The recession lessened the implied moratorium on discussing money, but only slightly. We urgently need to open the lines of communication, and that can often be accomplished by injecting a little tongue-in-cheek humor.

For example, consider the name of this chapter, "$aving Your Assets." This title was borrowed, in part, from one of my show segments on CNN called "Smart Assets." The segment's play on words alone served to break the ice and allowed viewers to be more open about the personal money issues they faced.

Everyone is entitled to his or her own money, whether it is earned, gifted or inherited. If it is *your* money, then take it personally. How you manage your assets says a lot about who you are. Your future and livelihood depend on how you make your money work for you.

As time passes, however, certain decisions will surely have to be made on how best to manage a loved one's assets. In order to do that successfully, you have to remove boundaries and perceived attitudes about money management *before* issues such as health or aging become critical variables.

How to discuss money with elders

Case in point: When my parents entered into the last year of their lives (they died six months apart) their health failed dramatically and quickly. My brother, ten years my junior, had predeceased my parents, so the job fell solely to me to broach the subject of my parents' finances. I loved my brother dearly, and in times of frustration in the process of managing their last days and then their estates, I would say to myself, "Where is my brother? He was younger. He should be here to help me get through this." While providing information on resolving these kinds of issues was part of my profession, it didn't make the process any easier.

It's hard emotionally to become a parenting child and face the fact that our parents, the people who reared us, grow old. In turn, they often require our assistance in ways that challenge our inner child. Discussing money with aging parents can be difficult. And when they push back about the forward progress you're trying to make on their behalf, what's an adult kid to do?

At the time, I was living in New York and they were in Las Vegas, after moving to what they thought would be an ideal retirement community for them. A few years before their relocation, my dad had been diagnosed with, and successfully fought, an aggressive melanoma. Then one day I received a call from Dad. In his unwaveringly gregarious style, he quipped: "My luck ran out in Vegas, Val. The melanoma is back." Not only was his melanoma back, it was back with a vengeance, requiring multiple surgeries and chemotherapy treatments.

At that point, I became a long-distance caregiver. Robert, my husband of 18 years, helped me relocate my parents to Tucson, Arizona. My mother, then 76, was more willing to talk about everything in their new circumstances, including finances. My father, the proud, 82-year-old retired U.S. Air Force lieutenant colonel, was less inclined. "I'll tell you when you need to know." This was his stock response to any questions dealing with money. He wanted to remain in charge and in control until he wasn't. He told me all the necessary paperwork was "signed, sealed and in a three-ring notebook" and that it would be given to me "when the time is right."

What I tried to relate to him, as I have done with so many others in similar situations, is that you can't plan under the premise that everything will be handled smoothly in an emergency. And unfortunately, it is often the opposite experience that occurs. That's why the time to discuss these understandably emotional personal matters is when people are of sound mind and body–which my parents, at this point in time, thankfully were. However, I knew that delaying conversations with me about their estate planning and retirement wasn't acceptable or prudent. I wrestled with how I would ensure that their estate plans and end-of-life needs were in order. I had to bridge the generation gap. What I realized was that no matter my age, I was still their child. I decided to tap into their lifelong commitment to me as loving, dedicated parents. I figured the best way to get them to show me *their* money was to show *them my* hand.

Icebreakers

I addressed the subject with my parents by telling them I was in the process of preparing my important personal papers and needed their help regarding dates, childhood illnesses, family health history and so forth. I first *assured them* that I was healthy and that there were no health issues that were causing me to prepare my will, but since I had relocated to a new state, I wanted my legal papers in order. They were immediately engaged because they perceived it to be about me and for me. That was the first of many incremental chats that ultimately became conversations about *their* health, money and end-of-life wishes.

As I explained to them my intentions as to how I wanted my assets distributed, they talked about how they wanted theirs divided – some to their grandchildren, some to other family members and so on. They began to look again at their money from a parental perspective and not a personal perspective. This was my icebreaker.

It was Mom who, just a few days after our initial conversation on estate planning and without ceremony or much comment, presented me with their three-ring estate-planning notebook. She told me to go make a copy of everything in it and return it before Dad got back from running errands.

Less than a year later, my father had a silent heart attack, was hospitalized and in grave condition. Three days after Dad, my mother suffered an acute gall-bladder attack and had emergency surgery. Prior to this procedure she had displayed slight confusion and memory loss, but after her surgery it manifested itself as full blown Alzheimer's. I was emotionally devastated. My parents were down at the same time and I was living 3,000 miles away. But at least I had a plan. It was their plan. I had the contents of their three-ring binder, which my mom had "gifted" to me months earlier with all their major decisions and documents. (I was doubly blessed. I found Dad's original binder under lock and key in their small safe.)

When dealing with such sensitive issues as your parents' pride, needs and financial security, you must be able to develop trust, and that is accomplished through sympathetic understanding. Because you cannot be in the heads of your loved ones, it is perhaps best to approach these complicated situations armed with Plato's words: "Be kind, for everyone you meet is fighting a harder battle."

Through love, and at times strained communication, my parents came to understand that like oxygen, money was among our common denominators. It doesn't define us, but it does remain a life force.

It is with this same approach that a 15-year-old grandson can teach his 75-year-old grandmother online banking or, conversely, a grandfather can teach his granddaughter the value of a hard-earned dollar.

Assigning Assets

We have to change the mind-set that "I got here first. I'm going to die, then my children and then their children." Though we know this isn't reality, our mind still processes it as if it were. For my generation, we need only look to the Vietnam War Memorial Wall in Washington, D.C., to know how life cycles are forever broken. People don't die in the order they arrive on earth. That's why everyone, regardless of age or health, must acknowledge death as a reality. With this realization, a legally binding plan for what happens to belongings, assets and wishes should be executed immediately.

I am the sole survivor of my nuclear family. At times, I was angry about having to make solo decisions regarding my parents' care and carry that weight alone. But I have had conversations with others who had to orchestrate similar parenting-child, end-of-life decisions with multiple siblings, all of whom had differing opinions about their parents' final needs and the money required to pay for them. Regardless your stage of life, there are no easy answers when trying to determine what to do with assets. In the final analysis, right in the midst of dealing with the heavy emotional loss of a loved one, we also have to deal with the business of death, dying and the money related to it.

In the process of life transitions and assigning assets, it is so very important not to hold your parents hostage for your memories of assumed assets, such as a childhood home. If they are still alive, but the home you grew up in is too much for them to handle, they should consider taking out a reverse mortgage (a special type of loan agreement designed for homeowners over 62 years of age). It provides access to the home's equity in cash payments, freeing up money they may use for other important expenses. The loan is repaid by means of relinquishing the home when the homeowner dies or moves.

Don't tell your parents, "You *can't* sell the family home!" Instead, put your money where your memories are. If you're enamored with the house of your childhood, offer to buy it from them. If you really mean it, set the plans in motion and get the purchase transaction done officially. Family members do not always cooperate. Everyone will not want the same things. Family relations, money and other assets are woven into an intricate tapestry. You can't start randomly pulling threads out (claiming money or other possessions from the estate) without a well-thought-out plan. You may not only ruin the image of the family tapestry but also reduce the overall value of your parents' portfolio.

Yes, end-of-life and estate-planning conversations can be difficult. But what happens if you're not prepared and you receive a call saying that a parent or loved one has died? Now what? In these tragic situations, people show how they feel. And when you show how you feel, and your heart is broken, you may become an unknowing victim of opportunists and even some good-hearted people: "We understand your loss and this is how we can help. We understand how much you loved this person, and this [product] will show it." They could persuade you to spend money you can't necessarily afford.

The State of the Estate Plan

If there's an estate plan, your mind will know the wishes and intentions of the deceased, which will make it easier for you to make necessary arrangements cost-effectively, expediently and confidently so that you are truly free to mourn.

I knew that my father wanted to be buried in Arlington National Cemetery. I had promised my parents they'd be buried together. But I didn't know whether that was allowed there. Nearly two years before my dad's death, my husband started orchestrating that request by working with the Veteran's Administration to better understand the rules and regulations for burial there. While my father fell ill before my mother, she quite unexpectedly died six months before he did. At her memorial service, it was with great comfort that I was able to let him know that not only had his wishes for his eventual interment at Arlington been granted, but that Mom would be there, too. With full military honors, the urn with their co-mingled ashes was buried at Arlington National Cemetery in Washington, D.C. On one side of the pristine white grave marker, my father's name is chiseled along with his military campaigns; on the other side, the words "Vivien A — His Wife."

There is something so very comforting and

satisfying about that accomplishment. I couldn't have reached that achievement without the help of an *accomplice* – my husband, Robert, who worked quietly and deliberately to help me attain their goal.

When matters of the heart and mind are interwoven with assets, it is critical that there is a trusted friend, a partner, by your side. This might be likened to a covert operation to afford you the kind of backup support you need without upsetting other members of the family during difficult times.

I'm a work in progress, as I believe we all are. After my parents died and I was able to begin to grieve, I approached my daughters so as to alleviate any related hardships down the line for them. It was easier to speak with them than it was for me to initially speak with my parents.

My daughters are both wonders and wonderful at what they do in their lives. But it became clear which daughter was more emotionally capable of handling the various aspects of my estate plan. This clarity came as a result of respecting their inherent personalities as well as having an open and honest discussion about who could handle what.

My grandmother gifted a legacy of strength and wisdom to my mother, who passed it along to me.

And I am simply transferring the same message – although defined more as it relates to assets – to my daughters. I am committed to creating these same traits in my grandchildren. Good money habits start early. Unfortunately, so do bad money habits, and they can be subconsciously passed along through the generations.

You may be the first generation in your family to commit to creating an estate plan. You have a choice to do it now, or do it later. When faced with the loss of your loved one, you want to be able to embrace the grieving process and begin coping with life without this person in it. The last thing you want is to be forced to make dollars-and-cents decisions at a time when life isn't making sense.

Know Your Self-Worth

There are different ways assets can be defined. While most equate wealth with money, it is important to understand that wealth is also subjective. It is not just dollars and coins. There are mental assets and skill sets that represent a value. Perhaps an employer or an investor will recognize these assets and compensate you accordingly.

When speaking to 20-somethings, especially those fresh out of college seeking their first job, I'll ask,

"How many of you will work for twenty-five dollars per hour?" Almost always, the majority of them raise their hands. I then ask of the minority who didn't, "How many of you would work for fifty dollars per hour?" Of course this group is more than happy to raise their hands for twice the amount. The first batch of responders will huff and puff saying, "Well, if I knew you were going to offer fifty, I would have waited."

I use this exercise because it demonstrates a point while engaging the audience. We have to be educated, aware and ready to expect that there is likely fine print in any offer. You have to know your self-worth.

Val-uable Money Mantra:
Know your self-worth by continually examining your financial portfolio.

It doesn't matter whether you are a low-income single mother, a college graduate, a middle-aged professional reentering the marketplace, or a widowed father with small children, you have to ask the question, "What do I need and why?" before you can answer the question, "What do I want?" Needs and wants are different. In order to be responsible for yourself and those who depend on you, you must learn to ask yourself the right questions before making money-related decisions.

Within you exists a little voice. When you are approaching decisions, listen to that voice. It might tell you to move forward or tell you that you need a time-out. And whether you are 5 or 50, you are never too old for a self-imposed time-out. So take a moment to understand what your existing assets are and how you plan to manage them.

Pay Yourself First

When I first started playing golf, the instructor told me over and over again to keep my head down. I thought it would be impossible to keep my head down while trying to swing and move the ball forward. Then she instructed me to pick *one dimple* on the ball and concentrate on hitting that exact spot. I thought: *The average golf ball has between 300 and 500 dimples – which one should I pick?* But her point, of course, was that I had to focus.

At any one time in our lives, we have hundreds of variables in constant motion, especially relating to money. When dealing with your assets, your focus should be on paying yourself first. This is another one of my mantras. With budgeted bills accounted for, this could mean promising that you will set aside five dollars each week in a retirement account. That might sound like a small amount, but this approach is better than a person who might say that they will set aside $500 a month when they have it. More times than not, that person never saves a thing.

Val-uable Money Mantra:
Pay yourself first.

While your asset-management strategy will depend on your age, income, existing assets, portfolio and tolerance for risk, increasing your overall wealth comes down to granting yourself options while maintaining discipline. When you have the discipline to pay yourself first, you are sending a message to peers, family members and employers that you are valuable. So each and every time you receive money, invest in your future. It has been said that time is our most important asset. With proper foresight, your assets will grow exponentially.

Specifically, by working with a professional you should dedicate time and energy to determine:

- **Tax Planning.** You may be able to reduce taxes on your investment income, minimize estate taxes and determine net-worth and cash-flow predictions.

- **Risk Planning.** You can protect family

resources by determining the amount of insurance you require to protect against property loss or death, the investment strategies that are best for you, and how medical care will be given in the event of illness, injury or disability.

- **Estate Planning.** You can ensure that wealth will be transferred according to the deceased's wishes, in a timely manner and with minimum tax liability.

This Little Piggy Is All Mine

I bought my first-born grandchild, Morgan, a "four pigs" piggybank – a mother pig with three baby pigs gathered in front of her. One pig was not enough, and I'll tell you why. Each pig is ready to be marked for a specific purpose. In Morgan's case, we chose "save," "spend," "share" and "invest." For an adult, this might equate to a "piggybank" for rainy-day funds, retirement or philanthropy. Each family has different wants, needs and goals, and saving for each separately is a discipline that should be instilled at an early age.

I told my grandlittles (Morgan's sister, Savannah, is 5 and has her own "four pigs" piggybank) that the big, momma-pig part of the bank was for them – that by saving, they were paying themselves first.

But the little baby pigs were theirs, too. They were encouraged to give them something every time they had money (usually loose change or the random dollar bill).

As these children grow they will have little jobs, such as lemonade-stand enterprises; they'll enter high school, go to college and get their first real job. And they will have grown up with the idea of compartmentalized saving. The four-pigs mentality can be easily adapted to bank and credit-union accounts. When my grandlittles eventually secure their first professional job that offers a 401(k) plan, their minds will have been conditioned to be part of this plan because they have always saved. From their perspective, the 401(k) represents one of their pigs, a long-standing metaphor for asset management. And yes, I always tell them to remember what Grandmom "GoGo" says: *It's your money so take it personally*®.

As a result, the bridge of knowledge comes into focus. On the one hand, my grandchildren are putting money in their pigs; on the other hand, not long ago by repetition, I convinced my dad that "getting money out of the wall" was a convenient and useful banking option. Teaching how to handle personal money and manage it well consistently, from one generation to the next, requires a never-ending cycle of communication, learning and shared growth. What money mantra might my grandchildren teach my daughters?

The $10,000 Question

Managing assets throughout life requires a committed mind-set so that you are prepared to make informed, lifelong money decisions. When I'm engaging an audience, for instance, I give the following scenario: "What if I offered each of you $10,000? You can do one of two things with it, but you can't split it. You can put the money toward your retirement or that same money toward your child's education."

I understand that not everyone has a child. But everyone has a child in their life, whether it is a niece, nephew, godchild or friend's child, so the scenario applies to all.

Whenever I ask this $10,000 question, at different gatherings across the nation, the majority of people who are parents usually offer to pay for the child's education. While there aren't many one-size-fits-all answers on how to handle money, there is one universal truth: If offered the aforementioned choice, always fund your retirement first.

As a parent, I completely understand the gut

response to help your children because I made this *mi$$ed-take* when I divorced. I thought of my daughters' education over my retirement. But the reality is that with your assistance the child can apply for loans or secure grants and scholarships to pay for college or other continuing education. They have time on their side. You don't. After all, who is going to give you a loan for retirement? If you can't afford to save for your retirement *and* your child's education, you have to make the smart, logical decision that will move you forward toward your goal – saving for retirement. This isn't a selfish move or mind-set. It's a smart and realistic decision. Kalman Chany, the founder and president of Campus Consultants, Inc. and author of many personal-finance books, including *Paying for College Without Going Broke*, says, "What most families don't realize is the most aid in grants, scholarships or loans goes to those who are the savviest applying for it, not necessarily those who are the neediest." I take his point to mean that you can allocate your *research* assets and figure out ways to help pay for a child's education (applying for state or federal grants, private scholarships, loans and so on) without breaking the bank or derailing your retirement savings.

In the end, if you don't prepare financially for

your retirement, you are in effect causing a systemic money problem within your family that will be passed down to the next generation, who may not be able to afford this *mi$$ed-take*. Again, this brings us back to the importance of setting and sticking to a budget. When you determine your discretionary spending and allocate it to various money goals and needs, you can better answer the question, "What you would do with a $10,000 windfall?"

Second Chances

What if you didn't have piggybanks, you haven't contributed to your 401(k) and you weren't magically given $10,000. Is it too late for you? No! The Greek philosopher Aristotle said, "All human actions have one or more of these seven causes: chance, nature, compulsions, habit, reason, passion and desire." I'm a firm believer in second chances and understand that the remaining six actions mentioned above have the ability to influence decisions in life – some for good and some resulting in *mi$$ed-takes*.

Second chances come in many forms: second marriages, second professions or a second chance at life after a health scare. While some people are creatures of habit, I think we have great capacity to change when inspired to integrate social, financial and familial life properly.

Val-uable Money Questions:
Could I outlive my money?
How much will inflation diminish my savings?
How do I pay my bills and still have money left over?
Do I control my money or does my money control me?
Is my net worth worthy or could I do better?

Over the past several decades, our society has changed. Today, people are more accepting of the idea that the family unit has shifted, including who makes the money and who manages the household. Similarly, with money-management issues there are second chances to take care of *mi$$ed-takes* that occurred in your past. The most important thing: Don't beat yourself up. Remember my dad's theory – look in the rearview mirror too long and you won't know what (opportunities) you'll run into.

Perhaps Emerson said it best: "Courage consists in the power of self-recovery." Asset management requires both of these critical components: courage and self-recovery. Collectively as a nation we are going through the latter. Respectively, moving forward, you have the courage to take control of you and your family's assets. Small changes add up. Small changes in how you think about your money do, too.

Chapter 4

Money, Honey

*"I have enough money to last me the rest of my life,
unless I buy something." — Jackie Mason*

The way in which people date today is fascinating.
Things have certainly changed over the years.
Nowadays, potential mates Google each other and
research pertinent information after a first meeting,
or often before meeting. (It's hard to have a truly
blind date these days!) Depending on what is
available online, you can form an opinion outside the
traditional first impression by viewing a Facebook
or LinkedIn profile or reading a tweet about random

likes or dislikes.

Social networking is the new status quo. So how can we be a society that has at its fingertips the ability to find out just about anything about someone, but when it comes to love, marriage and money, the last is treated like "we are not going there." When will we get over this money hump – the trepidation of asking smart questions about money issues that impact both parties' futures? It is as important as love. Before a couple – young or old – takes their relationship to the next level, each of them should pay closer attention to their respective finances before becoming a fiancé.

Val-uable Money Tip:
Couples, young or old, should pay close attention to individual finances before taking their relationships to the next level.

Too often I hear, "We can fix it later" or "I don't want to know now." This is especially true of young lovers who are approaching the critical decision of spending their lives together. For many, it seems that they hear financial advice the same way that Charles Schulz's *Peanuts* characters heard their teacher: *"Waa, waa, waa waa."*

To start out on the right foot, it is important that

the communication barriers surrounding money issues be systematically dismantled. As Irish playwright George Bernard Shaw said, "The single biggest problem in communication is the illusion that it has taken place."

Wedding Bells: A Financial Wake-Up Call

Planning a wedding can be exciting but overwhelming. For a woman, the details are seemingly endless. What kind of dress to wear? How much will the dress cost? What color should be selected for the bridesmaids' dresses, and will they match the groomsmen's vests? How to determine the seating chart? What type of flower arrangement will the tables have? The list goes on and on. But how often does the list include a visit to a financial planner? And perhaps a better first question: Who is going to be the couple's financial planner?

Financial specialists encourage couples to "know the score" – each other's credit score, that is – to eliminate misunderstanding about each other's financial circumstances. Those scores will impact *your* goals and habits moving forward. But more often than not, by the day of the wedding every other detail of the wedding plans is in order and this crucial step is left out.

Couples combine lives, hopes and dreams, but in the midst of that wonderful pursuit there often is a lot of dirty laundry to air out. This includes hidden truths about spending habits, savings, debts and real estate holdings, among other critical variables.

I am a romantic; it is my hope for every couple that their love grows and matures. But the honeymoon does end, and reality will set in. Couples entering into marriage or a committed partnership have a choice: Talk about money now or fight about it later.

Val-uable Money Tip:
You can talk about money now or fight about it later.

Generally speaking, men and women possess certain strengths and weaknesses when it comes to money management. These differences – in their approaches to saving and spending, for example – can be far-reaching. And when not addressed with proper communication, these differences are often troublesome. Katherine Hepburn once joked, "Sometimes I wonder if men and women really suit each other. Perhaps they should live next door and just visit now and then." Men and women hold different mind-sets when it comes to money. Communication is the bridge.

Often it is these inherent differences that when combined can create a winning balance. Over the years, however, traditional roles have changed, signifying and requiring new approaches to household management.

The Changing Role of Women

According to a report from the Pew Research Center titled "Women, Men and the New Economics of Marriage" (January 2010), a larger percentage of men are married to women whose education and income exceed their own. In 1970, 28 percent of married men attained a higher degree of education than their wives, while 20 percent of married women were more educated than their husbands. In 2007, the figures were nearly reversed, with 28 percent of wives being the more educated and only 19 percent of husbands. And women are contributing in greater numbers to household incomes. Before the baby-boom generation, many women didn't work outside of the home. Therefore, marriage more often enhanced the economic status of women than men. Over the past 30 years, however, economic gains associated with marriage have been greater for men than for women.

In 2007, the same Pew Research report found that the median household incomes of three groups

– married men, married women and unmarried women – were roughly 60 percent higher than those of their counterparts in 1970. But for a fourth group, unmarried men, the rise in real median household income was smaller – just 16 percent.

What do these figures signify? Women are bringing more assets to marriage than ever before. Should women commingle all of these assets with their partners' assets? Should assets cohabitate? Women have to remember that it is *their money* so they have to *take it seriously and personally.* They must make informed decisions that may result in certain assets remaining separate so that they are protected.

The following is a list of common characteristics the majority of women share when it comes to money management. Do any of these describe you?

- Women are exceptional investors.

- Women have a goal-oriented approach to investing.

- Women are relationship-oriented.

- Women place a high premium on trust.

- Women tend to use power and money to change communities, not just their own individual circumstances.

- Women tend to invest in the future emotionally and financially.

- Women tend to include young people and elders in the planning and use of personal money.

Men, many of whom are hard workers and high earners, often have a different approach to money than women do. For example, men normally have to be reminded, more than women, about the importance of having at least three to six months' worth of living expenses saved in an accessible emergency savings account. Conversely, men are likelier to express concern that they're in love with a woman who has a "shop until you drop" mentality that results in high, unpaid credit card debts and other less-than-desirable money-management issues. But men also have to address foreboding character flaws as it relates to their money. However special and strong the bond of love is, it should not deny anyone the right to individual economic stability. But so often it does.

White-Coat Syndrome

Couples should make sure they are of the same economic mind when they join forces and form a family unit. But many people would rather do anything other than discuss money matters. When considering seeing a doctor, some people suffer from white-coat syndrome, a phenomenon in which patients exhibit elevated blood pressure in a clinical setting but not in other settings. In short, it is a form of anxiety. Many people have a similar fear of taking the necessary steps to confront personal economic issues, especially when it comes to the heart of the matter: not wanting to make the person you love look or feel bad.

If you have poor money-management skills, you may experience hypertension and anxiety every month when bills are due – "It's the first of the month and here we go again." This state of mind is unhealthy emotionally, physically and spiritually as well as financially. Don't be afraid to confront your money-management issues and talk about them openly and regularly with your partner or spouse. It may take a while or yield only an incremental change, but consider money talks another form of family asset building.

In general, people mismanage their money not due to a lack of effort but because they are not equipped with financial know-how. This lack of understanding can be further magnified when entering a relationship like marriage. Money principles – the basics of home finances – aren't regularly taught at the family dinner table or in the nation's schools. Financial books and other tutorials often present complicated content that can only be appreciated by people who have long understood and built upon the basics. You are in charge of your money management. Money has no conscience. It depends on yours.

Val-uable Money Tip:
Money has no conscience. It depends on yours.

The thrill two people feel upon falling in love and starting a life together is often a magical moment in time. Being caught up in love is wonderful, but lingering in that mind-set can also lead to periods of denial about critical issues, such as – you guessed it – money. I have met with and counseled countless people who overrode their logical decision-making processes only to make bad financial mistakes because of love or because they were afraid of having a confrontation.

Warren Buffett once said; "Only when the tide goes out do you discover who's been swimming naked." The honeymoon period of a couple's relationship is the tide, and eventually the water recedes. Then you are left exposed, surrounded by truths you didn't see before.

With almost all major life decisions, making sound financial decisions can become compromised, especially when emotions come into play. It is imperative that, whenever possible, individuals pay down debts before entering a committed relationship, especially if they plan to combine money or share finances. So make a plan. When it comes to plastic, remember that paying the monthly minimum on your credit cards has never been a good idea. At current interest rates, it could take years to pay off the balance if you pay only the monthly minimum. Lingering debt places a great deal of pressure on your relationship. Do your due diligence before proceeding with your relationship.

One of my close friends, a producer at CNN, got married a few months before I joined the staff. Over the years, we developed a great friendship. I'm friendly with her husband, and their family now includes four children. Before they got married, however, she told her husband-to-be, "I will not marry you until you are debt-free." He did it because he loved her and respected her request. But how many people would have made that effort if not presented with a similar ultimatum?

Money Has No Conscience — It Depends on Yours
When financial questions are not asked of

potential partners, a tremendous amount of excess baggage is discovered – often at the worst of times. And just like how most airlines charge you per bag when you fly, when one enters into a committed relationship or marriage, you pay a price per "personal money history" bag. This is the business of money and marriage.

A detailed, open accounting allows each person to maintain his or her own financial thumbprint. This approach sets the platform for stability in the future in the event there is a job loss or a medical emergency. The family remains whole because there is another person with strong credit who can shore up loose ends and qualify for a low-interest loan if necessary.

The economics of marriage can't be overlooked. Before couples decide on a wedding date, they should give themselves a most valuable gift: a look at each other's credit report, followed by an appointment for a series of meetings *together* with a certified financial planner. It's in this environment that you can come to know each other's risk tolerance and savings mentality.

There are four types of savers. Which type are you?

1. **The planner saver:** a person who controls

spending and budgets to save.

2. **The struggler saver:** someone who has trouble staying afloat financially and finds it difficult to save.

3. **The denier saver:** a person who sees no reason for a budget because they don't see themselves in trouble financially.

4. **The impulsive saver:** a person who unfortunately spends money today like there's no tomorrow because his or her attitude is that tomorrow will take care of itself.

Source: Federal Reserve Bank of Dallas

Money Talks Matter

When I was a very young girl, I called my grandmother "Mudder." When I got excited, I shortened it to "Mudd." Over the years, Mudd's pearls of wisdom, which came to be known as Mudd-isms, made otherwise confusing concepts crystal-clear to me. She would often say that "97 percent of what you worry about never happens." This is tantamount to toeing the line between due diligence and anxiety.

Everyone's looking for financial wisdom right now. The first step is for each of us to admit that we haven't been good stewards of our money – or, if we have, that we haven't shared our knowledge both up and down our family's generations and among the communities in which we live to affect change.

To break down walls and open lines of *money* communication, couples should:

- Be open about finances and taxes.

- Consult each other before big expenditures.

- Review family money priorities regularly.

- Be sure that both of you know the location of all financial documents and passwords.

- Set a date for a monthly financial literacy conversation. Make known to other family members and friends your family's commitment to saving and responsible spending. Your state of mind regarding money can be an example and motivation to others.

- Confront financial challenges together. Knowledge is power, and a responsible spouse can help make a good financial plan that leads to recovery.

- Consider that at least 25 percent of today's labor force has elder-care responsibilities that can impact the finances of adult-child caregivers and their families.

- Consider that between 30 and 40 percent of workers will be assisting elderly parents in 2020, compared with about 12 to 25 percent in 2010.

- Remember that non-married partners have many of the same estate-planning mechanisms available to them as do married couples (wills, trusts, etc.).

There are certain shifts in thinking that come with growing older. Your 20s are a transition period. You're just out of college or trade school, trying to figure out what to do with what little money you might be making. Your decisions are usually associated with peer interests. You are likely living in your first or second apartment. It's a brave new world. At this time, you begin to realize what the term *recurring expenses* means, but that doesn't necessarily equate to properly managing your money.

According to *Brides* magazine, these days the average age for a woman to get married is 27, and the average age for a man is 29. So it's when we enter the fourth decade of life that money usually becomes more of a focus. You may be thinking about your career or starting a family. It may also be the first time that retirement is a reality because you are working with people who are 20 years your senior who provide a portal into the retirement mind-set.

It is during this time that 401(k) plans become topics of conversation, as do annuities, stocks and other assets, such as homes and cars – things that were once furthest from your mind. In your 20s you could talk yourself out of life and disability insurance, but in your 30s that internal argument doesn't hold water.

Val-uable Money Tip:
Yours, mine and ours.

I love trilogies. Thus, I love the number three. When couples come together, I believe they should have three money accounts: yours, mine and ours. I offer this premise for multiple reasons. First, it encourages couples to cooperate on shared money issues. The most important question is defining household income and what type of household you intend to create. Once the household income is quantified, a couple should next agree to contribute to the monthly budget (recurring expenses). This amount can be contributed equally or by percentage, depending on income. Figuring out the actual amount of this contribution is not as important as figuring out the discipline. Essentially you're paying yourself and your household obligations by paying your bills on time, every time, all the time.

Val-uable Money Tip:
Pay bills on time, every time, all the time.

Household contributions should be made by both husband and wife unless one is staying home full-time and managing the household. Salary.com found that in 2009 the average equitable salary for a stay-at-home parent was $138,095. That's a significant contribution to the household.

Couples considering having children should consult a good insurance broker to get term life insurance, which ensures that your family is protected in the event of the death of either parent. Term life insurance is relatively inexpensive (sometimes pennies a day). It's for a specific period of time, such as 10 or 20 years – usually the amount of time it takes to raise a family or pay off a mortgage. If something were to happen to either insured parent, the other would be financially compensated through that insurance for the loss of the spouse's contribution. Term life insurance can help you sleep easier at night. Setting aside money to pay the premiums might require removing an item, such as Saturday morning bagels and coffee, from your discretionary budget. Just remember, the key word in financial planning is *planning*.

The "D" Word

Divorce is the last word a person wants to hear when starting a new marriage. But there is no way to have an honest discussion about love, money and marriage without talking about it. And divorce lawyers say that money issues – not sex or infidelity – are the leading reasons for the demise of marriages.

According to the Forest Institute of Professional Psychology in Springfield, Missouri, 50 percent of first marriages, 67 percent of second marriages and 74 percent of third marriages end in divorce.

Age at marriage for those who divorce in America

Age	Women	Men
Under 20 years old	27.6%	11.7%
20 to 24 years old	36.6%	38.8%
25 to 29 years old	16.4%	22.3%
30 to 34 years old	8.5%	11.6%
35 to 39 years old	5.1%	6.5%

Source: www.divorcerate.org

The process of meeting with a financial specialist helps to answer questions regarding money triggers. Are you a spender? Is your mate a saver? Does one of you have an important goal in mind, such as buying a home in the next year, but the other is content to live in an apartment because spending money to travel is a priority? Is your true love faithfully contributing to a 401(k) account but you haven't started saving for retirement yet?

A premarital counseling session or two with a certified financial advisor will help you both get to the heart of the matter regarding love and money: You must get your own financial house in order before you say "I do." What better gift can both of you give to your marriage than full disclosure of your assets, debts and other liabilities?

Having this frank money assessment with each other isn't easy. But it is an essential requirement to the fiscal health of your relationship or marriage. Lay your financials on the table, including how much you each make annually and what you pay *for everything,* including car notes, student loans, credit cards, child support, manicures, rounds of golf and anything else that is a recurring expense in your life.

Your commitment to each other represents the fabric of your relationship woven over many years. Should you pull it apart strand by strand in a divorce by separating your friendships, shared experiences and shared assets, you won't be left with a whole cloth.

But if your marriage does end, look to the future instead of focusing on the rearview mirror or on how life used to be. Then you can begin to weave a new, stronger tapestry that illustrates lessons learned, aspirations and new goals. There are no easy answers when it comes to divorce, but I know for a fact that if you maintained your money as *your* money, in addition to having contributed to the family needs, you will be in better shape financially when approaching this highly emotional and personal deconstruction.

Before you seek out a specialist – perhaps a marriage counselor or, failing that, a divorce attorney – you have to *specialize* in understanding what you want *your* end result to be. Stick with your goals and be motivated by my mantra: *It's your money so take it personally*®. This approach also removes the possibility of operating from the dangerous premise that you've been wronged and someone has to pay.

Your lifestyle will likely change as a result of the divorce. Lavish vacations and high-end vehicles may no longer be practical if the idea is for you to be able to eventually retire and live comfortably. While every situation will have respective variables, you must be of the frame of mind that you are able to adjust and adapt.

If you applied the concept of yours, mine and ours during the honeymoon and through the marriage, your emotional, physical and fiscal approach will have made the dissolution of the relationship easier. If you have been minding *your* money over the course of the marriage – including an annual reassessment of your portfolio, and ensuring that all beneficiary designations are clear and accurate and that financial papers are being delivered to your correct address – you will be able to better weather this storm.

Not too long ago, my second husband and I relocated back to the San Francisco Bay Area, a location we know well and consider home. We have no plans to buy a house in the near future; instead we are opting to rent. When we do buy property, we do it individually, but it benefits us as a couple.

I advocate that individuals not wait to acquire assets such as real estate. Don't let a distant wedding date or some other milestone hold you back. If you are able, buy the property and build your portfolio. In the end, it will only make your future partnership stronger as it's an asset you bring to the marriage.

And if the marriage falls apart, *your* assets remain *your* assets. The intent of your portfolio and the content of your portfolio must stay on point to successfully reach your big-picture goals. Individual holdings can still benefit the family unit; it is not necessary to place your spouse's name on the deed. If at a certain point you wish to do so because it represents a progression in your relationship or for other personal considerations, that of course is fine. But within a marriage, each individual needs to maintain his or her own financial identity.

Q & A Session

Valerie interviews Edward Tanenbaum, tax and estate-planning attorney and partner in the New York office of Alston and Bird, LLP.

VCM: What are three questions young couples should ask a financial advisor or attorney before they get married?

Edward Tanenbaum (ET):

1. Should they purchase a home immediately in order to build equity, or rent a home or apartment? And if renting is appropriate, for how long?

2. When the couple is ready to purchase a home, how will they determine the maximum mortgage that they can assume? And what fraction of the purchase price should they expect to pay out of

their own funds?

3. What are the benefits to entering into a prenuptial agreement, and is the recommendation to enter into such an agreement dependent upon the amount of assets that they have?

VCM: What's the most overlooked issue by couples (young and older) who are considering combining their assets?

ET: Couples who plan to combine their assets usually do not consider the estate-tax and creditor implications, or the impact in case of a divorce. Quite often the overall estate-tax impact and the ability of creditors to attach the assets of the debt-free spouse can be lowered by keeping assets in separate accounts. Also, if a divorce occurs, separate property (such as property acquired by gift or bequest) that is not commingled will to some degree not be subject to the claims of the other spouse in many states.

VCM: What can non-married but committed partners do to allocate or arrange for transfer of assets to each other?

ET: Non-married partners have many of the same estate-planning mechanisms available to them as do married couples, such as wills and trusts that can be drafted to properly transfer assets to the surviving partner. The one benefit that a non-married couple does not have is the federal estate tax marital deduction (which allows a married couple to defer federal estate tax until the survivor's death), but the non-married couple can protect against the estate tax with life insurance.

VCM: What's the estate planning frame of mind needed for young couples and for divorcing couples?

ET: When embarking on estate planning, although a young couple should focus on how to lessen the estate-tax burden upon their deaths, the other primary focus should be on who will they appoint as trustee to manage their assets for their young children and who should they appoint as guardian to raise their children (the guardian and the trustee need not be the same person). If a couple is facing a divorce, and they have not entered into a prenuptial agreement, each spouse may want to take steps to do a new will that protects their intended beneficiaries after the divorce (should one spouse pass away before the divorce is finalized, the surviving spouse may still have a claim to a portion of the deceased spouse's estate).

VCM: How do you transfer assets when in a second marriage with children from previous marriages?

ET: When structuring estate-planning documents, if someone is married and he or she is concerned about the ability of the surviving spouse to manage assets or the possibility that the surviving spouse may disinherit stepchildren, the person may want to consider executing a will that leaves his or her assets in trust for the surviving spouse. If the trust is a qualified terminable interest property ("Q-TIP") trust – which is a trust that only benefits the surviving spouse while he or she is alive, gives the surviving spouse all of the trust income and distributes the remainder to the testator's intended beneficiaries after the surviving spouse dies – the trust will qualify for the federal estate tax marital deduction and, thereby, defer estate tax until the surviving spouse passes away.

When approaching love and all the wonderful aspects of your life it represents, keep in mind that love and money are not interchangeable. They can complement one another, but in order to keep your health and wealth, consider them mutually exclusive.

Jackie Mason's quote at the beginning of this chapter, "I have enough money to last me the rest of my life, unless I buy something," provides for a good laugh. But as the English proverb says, "Many a true word is spoken in jest."

Chapter 5

———ɯ———

Toddlers to Tweens: Lifetime Lessons in Money Management

"It is incumbent on every generation to pay its own debts as it goes. A principle which if acted on would save one-half the wars of the world." — Thomas Jefferson

There are more than four million babies born in the United States each year. When my grandchildren entered this world, I was elated. My grandmother meant a great deal to me, and I had long treasured the opportunity to become one. When they were born, I gave them a gift: 529 college-savings plans.

Regardless of upturns or downturns with my personal finances, I have pledged to make a regular but modest contribution to this fund. It was set up by my father before he died; I contribute every quarter. I intentionally chose a small amount that I knew I could maintain without compromising my own financial well-being. As the money in the 529 plans and my grandlittles grow, the slow, incremental savings mind-set that develops will place value on personal money management. The future is a gift we can give our children today. (In fact, my daughter Ciara taught Morgan to acknowledge my contributions to his 529 plan by saying: "Thank you for being (a) present in my future.")

What is a 529 plan?

A 529 college-savings plan is a way to make post-secondary education more affordable. It is an account into which people can deposit money to save for college and other higher education—related expenses. The funds grow tax-deferred. And if the money is used to pay for college or other higher education—related expenses directly, it is tax-exempt at the federal level and sometimes at the state level as well. Federally tax-free withdrawals can be made to pay for qualified educational expenses, such as tuition, room and board, and books, at any accredited college, university or vocational or technical program in the United States and at a number of institutions abroad.

While every state offers a 529 plan, plans differ from state to state. Although you must name a beneficiary when you open a 529 account, you may change beneficiaries, as long as the new beneficiary is a member of the same extended family as the original beneficiary. There are no income limits restricting who may contribute. Individuals can make a one-time contribution of $60,000 without incurring potential gift tax, provided they don't make another contribution for five years.

Source: Lightbulb Press, Inc.

Types of 529 Plans

Savings plans are similar to 401(k)s and IRAs. Your contributions are invested in mutual funds or similar investments. The plans offer several investment options from which to choose. Your account will go up or down in value based on the performance of the particular investments you select.

Prepaid plans allow the option to prepay all or part of the costs of an in-state public college education. They can be converted for use at private and out-of-state colleges.

Private-college 529 plans *(formerly known as independent 529 plans) are separate prepaid plans for private colleges.*

Source: savingforcollege.com

Did I pamper and celebrate each of my grandchildren? You bet! I regularly provide appropriate presents and treats. But I'm not the grandmother who walks in the door with the latest toy. I'm all about providing regular mini adventures. We all know that as little children grow and begin to learn, they're like sponges absorbing their environment. Each parent or guardian has the ultimate responsibility of teaching a child not only the difference between right and wrong but also the difference between *want* and *need.* When my grandlittles and I spend time together, I always look for opportunities to have educational fun. Counting something (or everything) provides endless play.

My friend and colleague, Dr. Brenda Wade, a psychologist whom I introduced in Chapter 1, says the importance of communicating with children on issues of money management can't be underestimated. She says, "We teach our kids to be polite and to say *please* and *thank you.* Well, that's how fundamental money is. So why would you not teach your kids about money? But most people don't."

Here is a story about the importance of early money education: One day I was traveling on the subway in New York, which I love to do because it is an experience in diversity. I'm always amazed when I consider how many different languages might be spoken in any one car and then multiply that number by all the subway cars in New York. Perhaps it is the global kid in me, but I find it fascinating. On this particular day, the subway car was rather empty. I was seated. A woman and a man near me were standing like seasoned straphangers. I was close enough to overhear their conversation. They appeared to be work colleagues. The woman was explaining that her son was recently fired. When the man asked why, she responded that he worked at a retail store and the cash register jammed and he was unable to calculate change without its aid. It wasn't his fault, she explained passionately; the cash register was broken. I was both appalled and saddened when I heard this excuse. Everything in me wanted to approach the woman and tell her that the greatest disservice she could do to her son was to make excuses for his inability to perform the job. Of course, a greater question presents itself. How was he hired in the first place when he lacked the defining ability of a cashier: making change? When it comes to building proper money-management skills, be sure to teach the importance of determining who is responsible and what that responsibility is.

Defining *Want* vs. *Need*

The beginning of money talks for me is the first time a child says, "I want." Does he or she, with those incredibly cute, beseeching, puppy-dog eyes, really *need* it? Or does he or she just really *want* it? This is a conversation you can begin having with toddlers at the age of 2 or 3, and it's okay if you have to wade through crocodile tears of protest.

These scenarios usually play out at supermarkets when a busy mother or father is shopping with kids in tow. They reach the checkout line. Strategically placed at the child's eye level are gum and candy. We've all either experienced this before or seen it while waiting to pay for our groceries. Choruses, rants and occasional tantrums: "I want ... I want ... I want."

One day while grocery shopping I observed a mother in her late 20s with two young children, one of whom was roughly three years of age. This child would speak clearly until he saw an object he wanted. He then began to utter increasingly loud grunts and groans. His mother was a trendy dresser, decked out in the latest knockoff Juicy Couture ensemble and carrying a faux Coach designer purse.

She half-heartedly tried to reason with the child

but, at nearly every turn, added whatever the object was that he wanted into the cart. The younger sibling, seated in the shopping cart, removed his pacifier, pointed to his brother and made similar sounds. This cycle of inappropriate behavior rewarded is being passed down from parent to child and from child to child.

What message is this sending? I have a problem with this behavior because it reinforces poor value judgments both in demeanor and actions. Under this premise, children will not be taught how to distinguish *needs* from *wants* or how to prioritize them.

You should address children in the same manner as you wish for them to act. From years of experience as a mother and a grandmother, I understand that there is no one-size-fits-all approach to parenting. However, when it comes to teaching young children money-management concepts, there are accepted guidelines that can be applied universally.

If we do not instill money-management techniques at an early age, we are creating a generation of debtors rather than a generation of productive individuals that develops wealth. How *wealth* is defined varies from household to household, but the concept and potential mind-set of wealth-building are universal.

There are ways in which children can be taught the importance of numbers with everyday tasks. When my granddaughter Savannah was a 3-year-old preschooler, her mom would ask while packing her lunch whether she wanted her strawberries cut in half. Savannah would often respond, "No, thanks. I want four pieces, please."

She helped pack her lunch box, which had a series of interlocking containers – toddler Tupperware – that could hold snacks (sliced strawberries, for example). Savannah would count as she filled the tiny container: one, two, three and four. Of course, this was very basic, but the repetition of counting small bites of food for lunch and snacks will become a familiar and concrete idea. As she grows, she will consistently be able to understand the concept and transfer it to counting pennies, nickels, dimes and quarters.

The idea is to build on these learning concepts, which include assigning value to the things in our life that we enjoy. For example, at bath time – which is frequently harried but usually fun – you could teach a child to count the number of toys in the tub and assign value to each by selecting his or her favorites. The concept is the same as counting coins with different values and putting them in a piggybank – and, eventually, depositing money into a savings account. Taking the toys out, caring for them and returning them to their proper storage place assigns value not unlike the way we assign value to investment assets.

Make learning the skills that are fundamental to money management, consistently fun and mental from an early age. Every time parents do that it's also an opportunity for them to renew, restore and retool their own money-management disciplines. Take every opportunity you have with your child to count or measure. I did this many times when cooking or baking with my children when they were growing up, and I do it now with my grandlittles. I line up all the measuring cups. At a young age, children don't necessarily need to know the differences between a quarter, a third, a half and a whole. Fill up one cup randomly with rice or beans and let them pour the content into the different cups. Forget about the mess, because it happens. Children soon figure out what is too little or too much. It reinforces that there are values and measurements for everything. Subconsciously, they will take these lessons with them as they grow.

Just as the 529 plan is a gift for a child's future, the present moment is also a gift. We need to figure out how to teach children the importance of responsible short-term gratification. Grandparents, particularly, can become more relevant in this effort by being more deliberate in how they choose to contribute to their grandchildren's financial well-being. That might mean making a deposit to a grandchild's 529 plan on birthdays. Or it might mean buying something that a grandchild *needs,* like new shoes, as opposed to something a grandchild *wants,* such as another video game or pair of designer jeans.

The Age of Reason

In 1976, child psychiatrists Theodore Shapiro and Richard Perry published an article titled "Latency Revisited: The Age of Seven, Plus or Minus One." Many scholars, doctors and educators call this the "Age of Reason" because that's when a child develops a newfound sense of right and wrong. The article explained that children at this age are no longer focused simply on not getting caught or displeasing adults. They have the ability to identify with their parents' or other primary caregivers' expressed values.

Over the course of history, this age has been deemed a rite of passage. Psychologists conclude that the child's brain is able to reason, identify problems and understand consequences. Children can classify orders of operations and understand cause and effect.

As these changes are occurring, children begin to assign real values to money. Some children do it better than others. I have marveled at stories I have either covered or read about in which a child will take his or her "life savings" and donate it to a less fortunate family or to relief efforts supporting victims of a catastrophe. At the ages of 7, 8 and 9, children are incredibly intuitive. What was once a "mine, mine, mine" mind-set has morphed into a welcome understanding of socialization.

I was surprised to learn that when my grandson Morgan was about 7, he and his male classmates showed trust and friendship by sharing and loaning their favorite toys in an almost bartering fashion. They were not told to do this, but of course it makes perfect sense: With so many toys in any one child's possession, they have taken to exchanging toys with friends for periods of time. And though there is no paperwork or record, ownership is never lost or confused. This presents a perfect opportunity to discuss, for example, the dollar savings Mom and Dad are realizing because the child is sharing rather than asking for them to purchase the same toys.

Children are curious and will always want to try everything and anything they can. When they begin to realize the difference between items they *want* (and borrow or buy when on sale) as opposed to items they *need* (and often take for granted), they achieve a new understanding of value.

And when these communication lines are open, it may be a good time to discuss the concept of an allowance. Regardless of your personal stance on the issue, as a parent or guardian you will have to face it at some point. Some parents base an allowance on household chores; others treat it as a salary for being a member of the family. Here is yet another scenario where one size doesn't fit all.

Openly discussing the concept of an allowance is beneficial to all family members, Dr. Wade told me. "The reason we don't have these conversations easily or readily is because we have a lot of embarrassment and guilt about money," she said. She explained that money-related issues are often passed down from generation to generation and can include feelings of loss, shame, guilt or anger that haven't been resolved.

When it comes to allowance, I prefer a reward-based system. This allows the parent to be more thoughtful as to how to assign value to chores or contributions to the household. I didn't pay my daughters to wash the dishes because I wasn't paid to cook the meal. My daughters didn't leave their dishes on the table and my grandchildren don't leave their dishes on the table, either. They walk their dishes and glasses over to the sink. Sure, we had a few dropped and broken plates, but a message has been instilled regarding the value of being a member of the family unit: cooperation. There is also a value associated for those things they do that go beyond the call of duty for which they can be compensated.

The compensation model depends on your family income and budget. It could be a dollar amount equal to the child's age or a dollar per week. This formula could be a stretch for some families and acceptable for others. The benefit of providing a child with an allowance is that it gives them an opportunity to manage their own money. Otherwise, they are constantly positioned as a salesperson pitching you their *wants* or *needs.*

It Doesn't Have to Be the Terrible Tweens

Eight- to 12-year-olds are a fascinating demographic. By 2020, the U.S. Census Bureau estimates that this age group will number approximately 23 million. We needed only look to the White House to see the nation's First Tweens, Sasha and Malia Obama. When President Obama and family moved there in 2008, Sasha was nearly an 8-year-old and big sister Malia was looking forward to turning 11.

What do most tweens consider cool?

Music, Going to the movies, "Being smart", Video games, Smart phones, Social networking, Sports, Fashion, Supporting causes (environmentalism, etc.)

Put research, facts and figures aside for a moment. When I think about this age group, I tend to look to nature for a reference point. At this age, life is frenzied. Tweens' bodies are changing, hormones inform behavior, and junior high or high school is upon them.

Not unlike the age of reason, the ages of 12 and 13 represent another rite of passage for many religions and philosophies. In Judaism, for example, 13-year-old boys "come of age" after studying for and celebrating their bar mitzvah. Jewish girls, on the other hand, come of age at 12 after studying for and celebrating their bat mitzvah.

The tween demographic is a powerful but not easily defined group. Parents today are confused and troubled – in some respects, more so than in previous generations – because of technological advancements like smart phones and the Internet. Because every generation will compare their experiences to the experiences of the generations that follow, in the end, there is almost always a gap of thought.

To provide clarity, I spoke with a new friend, Brianne, a bright, intrepid 15-year-old, who gave her insights into the tween/teen mind-set. "It's probably harder to be a tween or a teen today than it was when my mother was that age because there is so much technology. She didn't have cell phones, e-mails or IMs and now we do. For tweens and young teens, it is just harder to keep up with everything."

Advertisers are gearing products to this tween demographic, using sex and sexiness like never before. Ad campaigns and marketing symbols that use inappropriate clothing for tween or younger girls are grossly irresponsible. These ads assign *value* to all the wrong things.

Tweens are a vulnerable demographic. So the adults in their lives need to make a concerted effort to rein in their spending and thought patterns with regard to what they *want* as opposed to what they *need.* Your tween's desire to keep up with friends and peers, much like money, requires oversight. Nobody has all the answers, but parents or guardians should ask insightful questions.

Dr. Wade notes that when tweens process money-management issues, their state of mind is often derived from learned behavior in the home and with peers. She continues, "Life is a neurological event. The brain isn't complete until age 24. The neurological reality is that a tween's frontal lobe of the brain doesn't function in a clear enough way yet. The frontal lobe is where high-level thinking is done and where consequences are understood. Until these tween kids can do that, it's the parents' responsibility to instruct them to make responsible money choices."

The tween market equates to approximately $335 billion per year. Marketers advertise ferociously toward this demographic because they understand that their tactics increase the burden on parents, who are faced with fending off the out-of-control spending habits of their child's conspicuously consuming peers. Parents and guardians should see this time in their child's life as a unique window of opportunity to speak with their tweens about money management – before bad habits are developed.

Let's say a tween approaches a parent about getting a cell phone. Automatically, money alarm bells should sound, and for good reason. In 2009, a

13-year-old girl ran up $5,000 in charges in one month for sending approximately 20,000 text messages! When dealing with your tween child, you can use this extreme case to your advantage. If your child has an allowance of $10 per week, ask your child to figure out how many weeks' allowance it would take to pay off a $5,000 bill. The idea is to put these concepts in a realistic, understandable formula. Most children will not be this extreme with their texting. But even if a managed cellular plan costs $50 per month, the child will realize that his or her allowance won't even cover that cost. This leads to an important question: Where does the money come from to pay for these things? Again, take the opportunity to explain the importance of working hard and the concept of creating and sticking to a budget. Always assign value to the object that's being discussed.

Tweens, like adults, are different in the way they approach money management. I was impressed with Brianne. When we spoke, she was 14 years old and eagerly anticipating her eighth grade graduation, which included a present from her parents: her first cell phone. This was her parents' signal to her that she was ready for the responsibility that goes along with being a high school student, an exciting milestone in her young life. What struck me was that she approaches money management logically and connects the dots along the way.

"I didn't used to think about what things cost. Now when I go shopping, I might see a blouse or a shirt I like but look at the price tag and if it is too expensive, I say to myself, *Never mind.*"

Brianne, who doesn't receive an allowance but is occasionally compensated for babysitting her brothers, continued: "As kids, we don't really know what a car or house costs, but if we have twenty dollars that is a lot of money. I know twenty dollars isn't really that much [money], but when I look to buy something, I think about it because I don't want to spend all my money [at once] and see it all gone."

During the tween and teen years, it is important that boys and girls earn an income in some fashion outside the home (unless there is a family business for which they work and are compensated). Similarly, this is a perfect time to begin to involve children in family finances. That way they can begin to equate value to everyday expenses, such as groceries, electric bills, automobile insurance bills, and the mortgage or rent.

I suggest scheduling monthly meetings. For example, the first Saturday of each month at 10 a.m.,

the family meets to pay bills. When children have
a firm understanding of the family budget, it helps
them to better interpret their *wants* and *needs* and how
they relate to the overall budget. By opening these
lines of communication you are sending the message
that they are capable of assuming money-related
responsibilities.

I thought I would run this concept by Brianne,
as tweens and teens are often busy. Between her
scholastic schedule and sporting events, her days
are filled with homework – and, she conceded, the
occasional two-hour gab session on the phone with
friends. The concept of a monthly family meeting
intrigued her. She suggested, however, that Sunday
afternoon was the best time to meet.

"As a family, we really don't discuss money
that much, but sometimes we do. I actually think a
monthly meeting would be good because I could see
what bills cost compared [with] my twenty dollars.
If we saw what the electric bill was, we [my two
brothers and I] could try and turn off more lights and
see next month if any money was saved." She added,
"It would be helpful for us kids (peers and siblings) to
know what two hundred dollars, for example, buys in
the real world as opposed to what we think in our kid
world."

It is through this process that parents can learn from children. Money flows up and down; therefore, we can learn and teach up and down money awareness. The importance of communication about money-management issues should be your paramount concern.

Val-uable Money Tip:
Money flows up and down; we can learn up and down.

I was traveling with a friend in the San Francisco Bay Area. She received a phone call while we drove. She put on the speakerphone. It was her college-age daughter, who immediately launched into a quandary over where she would spend spring break. Both destinations were outside the country. After the call, I asked my friend if her daughter presumed that the trip would be paid for by her parents. The answer was yes. While this might work for some families, this approach can also create a mind-set that could creep up and haunt you into the future. The presumption of such extravagances shakes my *dollars-and-sens*ibilities.

Don't Live in a Plastic World
The problem with this presumptive mind-set is that when otherwise-good kids are not taught the importance of assigning value to money, they could be faced with decisions that can adversely impact

their financial future.

Case in point: Until recently, when 17- and18-year-olds arrived at college, they were inundated with offers of free T-shirts and Frisbees, which were nothing more than promotions from credit card companies. Students signed up and left with meaningless gifts and a credit card – but no clue about how to manage it. Now that the Credit Card Accountability, Responsibility and Disclosure Act has taken effect, credit card companies are prohibited from pursuing college students so aggressively.

How bad had the situation become? In 2009, Sallie Mae, a college-financing company, conducted a nationwide survey that found that the average undergraduate carried $3,173 in credit card debt, which was the highest level since the company began collecting data in 1998.

But of course this problem often starts at home. And it can become systemic when younger siblings see their older brother or sister with one to three credit cards, each with a $2,000 line of credit. The parent or guardian has to step in and set a new course before it is too late. Oftentimes, however, what younger siblings overhear are parents complaining about their overspending college student without applying stop-gap measures. The younger siblings then begin to devise ways in which they will be able to get away with the same behavior when their time comes to leave home and attend school. This perpetuates poor money-management skills within the family.

Many kids, unfortunately, don't conceptualize that using plastic can lead to significant problems. They don't see it as credit or real money that's been spent at a very high annual percentage rate, or APR. Students and plastic are yet another example of unprotected spending. A prophylactic measure is required to protect against over spending. Yes, think prophylactic! I will say this over and over again, even though the term upsets some parents because it usually conjures the thought of unprotected sex.

Part of understanding the problem of overspending and how to control it requires that each person at this age be surrounded by what's often referred to as a *money posse,* a select group of friends who pride themselves in being efficient, committed money managers. By association, they can help guide and influence their fellow young protégé toward smart money choices and reinforce the proper frame of reference, that all credit cards *aren't* bad. When used properly, credit cards can be instrumental in building a favorable credit history.

I'm a proponent of prepaid cards, and I used them when I sent my daughters to college. These are simply branded cards (e.g., VISA, MasterCard and American Express) that are preloaded (and able to be reloaded) with a certain amount of money. They're used like a credit card but managed more like a checking account. The leading benefit is that because you're not borrowing money, you do not need to worry about finance charges, late charges or over-limit fees.

Although prepaid cards are beneficial, this is a cottage industry in which new features from the card company potentially carry related charges. Many prepaid cards have fees to activate ($10-$30), to reload or add money ($3-$5), to use ($10 a month) and even to cancel ($10-$15). These fees aren't always easy to find in the card agreement, but the charges will definitely find their way to your card balance, and many parents and college-age children don't read the fine print. Prepaid cards should be a stepping stone that teaches account-balance management. This approach prepares a college-age young adult for the responsibilities of owning and using a traditional credit card.

What's the alternative to not having discipline

when first establishing credit? Students eventually graduate from college with deep credit card debt and the unprotected-spending mentality that got them there. They can't pay off the bills and support themselves, so they often move back home. More bills are created for the parents, most of whom are approaching retirement and trying to save enough money to afford it. Unprotected spending is a vicious cycle best broken through education, starting as early as age 3. Everyone needs to practice the mantra *It's your money so take it personally*® for life.

Just as divorce lawyers cite money as the leading cause for the break-up of marriages, money issues within a family unit can forever alter familial relationships. While likely there will be no bloodshed, Thomas Jefferson is right when you apply his words to family money management: "It is incumbent on every generation to pay its own debts as it goes. A principle which if acted on would save one-half the wars of the world."

Chapter 6

———ɯɯ———

Stepping Stones Before Milestones

"I got my start by giving myself a start."
— Madam C.J. Walker

As the tween and early teen years are survived, it's important to establish new rules and to understand how to take calculated financial steps that will ensure a secure future. For 20-somethings, this is the perfect time to build a financial foundation.

Hindsight provides clarity. Parents and guardians, some of whom are baby boomers like me, are positioned to explain money-related differences to children and grandchildren by drawing parallels that encourage a thrifty, frugal, value-minded approach to adulthood. In addition, these parallels can connect them in a healthy, meaningful way to the mentality of the post — Great Depression generation.

Our modern-day recession had all the sights and sounds of a depression – we just didn't call it that (although some did refer to it as the Great Recession). It's our obligation to remind the generations that follow us – Generations X and Y, as well as Gen Z, those born in the 1990s onward – that nothing is promised, that life and security can be fragile.

In many cultures, entering into adulthood comes with great responsibility. In Japan, for instance, the age of majority is 20 (or 19, in some cases, depending on the actual birth date). People under 20 are not permitted to smoke, drink or vote. After their 20th birthday, however, they attend a coming-of-age ceremony known as *Seijin Shiki,* which is held on the second Monday of January. During the ceremony, all participating men and women are brought to a government building, where they listen to respected speakers, not unlike a graduation ceremony. At the conclusion, gifts, including money, are given to the new adults as they walk boldly into their respective independent lives. Rites of passage like this one highlight the importance assigned to preparing our young men and women for their future.

No More Baby Steps

For many college graduates, being in debt is a sobering reality. So it is important to be sure they understand that there are two kinds of debt: good debt and bad debt. An example of good debt is college loans. Although the average college graduate carried $23,200 in loan debt in 2009, that debt represents an investment in the future. Students seek higher education for knowledge – a degree – that will improve their lives.

And while it is imperative that student loans are repaid, the loan payments can be deferred for a period of time, if necessary. Any loan taken out after July 1, 1993, can be deferred if the recipient is returning to school at least half-time, is unemployed or is experiencing a financial hardship. Other criteria include participating in a graduate fellowship program or being enrolled in rehabilitation training.

Understanding what is available to assist with financial planning, such as deferment, is critically important. Those who meet these requirements should take the opportunity to defer payments and focus on clearing bad debt, such as credit card balances. Pay down the bad debt before focusing on eliminating the good debt.

Young adulthood is a period of significant change. This age group's greatest advantage is time. But often they make poor decisions, such as running up credit card debt. Such *mi$$ed-takes* are common, but if you make them, they can be easily remedied by changing your approach to spending and saving.

I have a young friend, Cory. She was raised in an affluent community where most children were given anything their hearts desired. Her parents (my longtime dear friends) gave Cory and her sisters everything they *needed* but not everything they *wanted*. They were taught a clear distinction between the two. Growing up, Cory learned the value of hard work by completing weekly chores. Upon successful completion, she and her sisters were each rewarded with a $20 allowance.

I have great affection for Cory and her sisters, and I have always lent my ear or made myself available to them. When she was about 25, I received a call – she was having financial problems. Cory, then a freelance talent coordinator and publicity representative in the music and commercial production industry, explained that she had completed a two-month project for which she wasn't paid. In order to do the job, she lived off her credit cards for two-plus months and was nearly $20,000 in debt. She told me, "I wasn't just up a creek without a paddle. I was clinging to the raft!"

She knew the value of a dollar, but she was now faced with tough decisions on how she was going to pay off her debt. This overwhelming dilemma led to a financial epiphany. Cory no longer wanted to live in fear and was exhausted from always wondering how she was going to make ends meet. She made a goal to pay off all her debt in one year. As soon as she made her decision, a silver lining appeared around her otherwise dark financial cloud. She was offered a position as an event manager for a VIP ticketing company. The money was good, and the new position required that she be on the road working with bands and entertainers for one year.

I was very pleased to hear her news and wished her all my best. Less than a year later, I received an e-mail from Cory. She was writing from Saskatoon, Canada, while on tour with a band. She wanted to let me know that she had managed to pay off two credit cards, saved $13,000 and estimated that she was six months away from paying off her car loan.

Now 29, Cory says her life on the road has

disrupted her plan to be a homeowner by age 30. Her new timeframe is "once the housing market stabilizes and I decide it's time to settle down," she told me via a text from her tour stop in Japan. She says that her diligence regarding saving money will allow her to do that.

Cory continues to use her debit card for all purchases she would have otherwise made with her credit cards. If she can't afford it, she doesn't buy it – which, she reminds herself, is a lesson that was part of the disciplines she learned growing up: *need* as opposed to *want.* Though credit card debt still is part of her life, she says: "The structure I set up several years ago of paying it down religiously has kept my head above water and my heart free from debt stress." Now much of the money she once paid toward debt – approximately half her salary – is directed toward retirement and investments (a Roth IRA and mutual funds).

The "B" word continued

You can't get out of debt if you keep spending. Setting and adhering to a budget should be a priority at any age. For people in their late 20s, like Cory, it is a perfect opportunity to make smart money choices that will help fortify their financial foundation and future. It is never too late or too early to get a financial life!

Val-uable Money Tip:
You can't get out of debt if you keep spending.

When conversations about money come up, many people intone, "I can't wait to get *back to normal*." Stop! Please don't say or even think that. Remember: The way we were and the way we handled money in the past are what contributed to the deep recession we experienced. Instead of back to normal, everyone needs to create and practice a "new normal" regarding money. That "new normal" begins with remembering the basics: You can't get out of debt if you keep spending. And you're more likely to keep spending if you don't make a plan to control it. That's why you should plan on making a *budget* your new best friend.

Before you throw up your hands and fall victim to memories of failed past attempts at creating a budget, try this: At the start of the upcoming month, take a pen and paper (or make a quick file on your smart phone) and record every single purchase you make. Just list the amount and what it's for. At the end of the month, highlight those expenses that are mandatory, such as rent, car payments, groceries and cell-phone bills. The remainder (the total of whatever expenses *aren't* highlighted) is your discretionary money. You may discover, for example, that you are spending upwards of eighty dollars per month on your daily doses of chai tea or latte. At this point, you can determine to cut the intake by half (or brew your own morning cup of coffee) and apply those forty dollars to pay down credit card debt. Having a budget (also known as a spending plan) also helps you determine when you use a debit card instead of a credit card.

Cory's use of her debit card is smart. Debit cards are great as long as you do the math regularly. When it comes to debit cards, it's important to keep track of your checking account and stay on top of balances and purchases. Again, the concept is basic, but many people find themselves in a debit dilemma because they forget to take this critical step. It's a good discipline to think of debit cards this way: You're paying *now,* whereas with credit cards you're paying *later.* To use your debit card means you have to have money in the bank *right now* to cover your purchase.

Once your credit cards are paid off and you exhale as you become free from plastic debt, don't cut them up and throw them away. Hold on to them (or at least the one you've had the longest). This is a credit-building tool. Practice making less-frequent purchases and paying the bill in full when you do. Your credit score in part is based on credit lines you have maintained over time. Use the system to your advantage!

Returning to the Nest

Most graduating college students' goal (or that of any person in their 20s) is to live an independent life. But the average debt for this age group makes this a hard objective to reach. According to the Bureau of Labor Statistics, in October 2009, 15.6 percent of 20- to 24-year-olds were unemployed, compared with 8.7 percent of people over the age of 25. A recent Pew Research Center survey found that 13 percent of parents with grown children say that one of their adult sons or daughters has moved back home in the past year. This boomerang-kid statistic was magnified during the recent recession.

According to the 2010 Monster College Survey from Monster.com, college graduates understand that they will have difficulty finding a job, and 52 percent (versus 40 percent in 2009) are moving back to their parents' house. Of the 1,250 recent college graduates polled, 31 percent say they expect to stay with their parents longer than one year.

Parents who allow their adult children to return to the nest must have rules in place even before the bags are unpacked. And while most parents' position is, "you always have a home," the fact is that for many married couples once the initial "empty nest" feeling fades, they focus on redecorating rooms and concentrate on quality partner time. Parents might be just as surprised to have an adult child return home after a four-year absence as the adult child who finds him- or herself returning due to limited options.

Ground rules should include having your adult child pay rent or some other regular, preset financial contribution to the household. The amount should be determined case by case, but the point is that there should be no free ride. Everyone must pull his or her own weight by contributing monetarily. But parents have to treat adult children with respect. They can't stay awake until two o'clock in the morning waiting for their adult child to get home on a Saturday night. A new dynamic is required, especially if the young adult and parents agree that the living situation is to be a stepping stone to independent living. So before the adult child moves back, parents and child must agree on a date when the adult child will leave. Should valid circumstances necessitate a longer stay, renegotiate a new departure date.

If a boomerang adult child needs to borrow the car on a regular basis, make him or her pay for a percentage of the insurance or car payment. By cohabiting, everyone is commingling, which requires a new approach to adult child/parent relationships. Parents and adult children should open the lines of communication and determine rules, guidelines, actions and attitude. The only way goals can be attained is if they are set in the first place.

Past Lives: Claiming Your Assets Then and Now

Progressive 20-somethings who are serious about their financial future are paying down debt and saving and investing their money. You, too, must take a long view of your financial portfolio.

Several years ago, I was working on a story investigating the estimated trillions of dollars that sit unclaimed in state treasuries. The reporter in me was skeptical, and it piqued my interest. After the story aired, I did a personal search that revealed I had 100 shares of long-forgotten stock dating back to 1969. At first I was shocked, then I reasoned that sometimes the hustle and bustle of life can eclipse past memories. So I thought back to that time period.

In 1966 I was a student in my junior year at San Jose State University, pursuing my degree in journalism. Freshly transferred from a tiny Montana college of several hundred to a student body of nearly 22,000 at San Jose State University in northern

California, I figured the best way to meet new people was to sign up for a much-advertised event called "rushing" a sorority. I soon learned that I was the first African American woman to do so. A few hours after returning from various sorority rush receptions, I was sitting in my dorm room when I received a call from the front desk. "You have male visitors," I was told, "Four of them!" I arrived at the dorm reception room and was greeted by four handsome young men. Two were dressed in suits and the other two wore white shirts, ties and letterman-type purple and gold sweaters with large Greek letter insignia. They rose in unison, introduced themselves by name and told me they were members of Omega Psi Phi fraternity, which was the only African American fraternal organization on campus. They explained that they were there to escort me to all rush activities to ensure my safety. I was, they told me, creating quite a stir on campus, and that the white sororities thought I was a member of the Student Nonviolent Coordinating Committee (SNCC) and a "radical" member of the NAACP – a test case there to cause trouble or unrest.

I went through the rush period always escorted to and from events by at least one of the Omega Psi Phi brothers. I was stunned, because I was simply looking for new friends. But I was grateful for the concern shown by these four visitors.

At the conclusion of sorority rush week came what was described as "the biggest upheaval ever" to disrupt the sorority membership meetings. Several sororities' national offices threatened to pull their chapter's charter if they pledged me. All these years later, a member of one of those sororities, who has remained a dear friend, said this issue was recently raised following an event I attended along with some of her sorority sisters.

"I was surprised when your name came up and they talked about the horrible experience of your rush. They have lots of hurt about it that has not healed," she told me. "There are still hard feelings about it. They still feel terrible about not being able to pledge you."

Many other longtime friends from that SJS Rush 1966 are nearer to me now that I've relocated back to the Bay Area. The memories are vivid and the experience made us stronger. As a result of that trying sorority rush experience, I developed and maintained meaningful relationships with members of Omega Psi Phi. I later pledged Delta Sigma Theta, a black sorority, among whose members were the late Dorothy Height and Lena Horne.

Over the next two years of college, I became the anchor for *SJSU Reports*, the daily five-minute television news program that aired on the local commercial station, and the school's first black homecoming queen.

During my senior year, a nationwide search was launched to find one college student to represent all college coeds across the country. Omega Psi Phi nominated me. I later won the National College Queen Pageant. It wasn't a beauty pageant. There wasn't swimsuit modeling or a talent competition. The pageant was based on finding a student who was well-rounded academically, civically and socially. I was the first African American winner. I was awarded a 1969 Firebird (brown with gold leather interior), a $5,000 wardrobe and 100 shares of Corn Products International stock furnished by the pageant's sponsor, Best Foods. Nevertheless, it was still a pageant. I had to wear sashes and tiaras. In fact, they gave me 15 tiaras to make sure I was never without one.

I traveled all over the nation making appearances. I was on *The Mike Douglas Show* and *The Dating Game*. I was taken to the Best Foods kitchen and taught how to create new recipes and cook meals. At that time, even women who were considered accomplished still had to go through the gauntlet of the perceptions and expectations of what it was to be a woman: cooking, cleaning, doing makeup and preparing a home.

It was a difficult period in our nation's history, especially if you were an African American woman in the public eye. As I traveled the states, including through the South, I received death threats. The passengers were cleared from a plane on which I was about to fly because of a bomb threat. When I arrived at certain hotels, they wouldn't let me through the front door. They later explained that because I was black they thought I was the help. I was wearing the tiara and sash that clearly showed I was the person for whom they'd been waiting! It was a painful time. But from this adversity I found enormous inner strength.

With these experiences, I became even more direct and deliberate in my actions. I reflected on what my parents said to me as a teenager in Montana, where I was the only African American in my school. They always asked, "What lessons can you learn from this?" I asked that of myself when as a cheerleader for my high school I was booed off the court by shouts of hurtful racial slurs. I held my head high then, as I did as the College Queen and as I still do today. My parents always said, "Own your experiences."

The College Queen experience was another representation of the rearview-mirror cycle: Here is where you are, here is where you have been and here is where you're heading. The following year, while serving my term and fulfilling pageant duties, I pursued and completed my master's degree at Columbia University's Graduate School of Journalism. My advisor was the legendary Fred Friendly, the man credited with producing the television shows featuring Edward R. Murrow, the journalist who dared to uphold freedom of thought during the time of McCarthyism.

Yes, sometimes the hustle and bustle of life can eclipse past memories. But losing track of that 100 shares of Corn Products International stock turned out to be a blessing. Once found, it was truly a significant windfall. For 20-somethings, I hope relating this story demonstrates that no matter your diligence, over the years it's easy to forget valuable items contained within what becomes your financial portfolio. I did. So can you. As a result of my unclaimed-property search, I found financial assets and revisited priceless (although painful) emotional memories.

Pay It Forward

For those young 20-somethings who are living on

their own or with roommates, paying down debt, and serious about their financial future, investing is the next logical step.

We all need a financial vehicle that has growth potential that either keeps up with or surpasses inflation. Investing at a young age allows you to place your money in aggressive portfolios. What's even better is that due to the recent recession, stocks of trusted, successful companies have essentially been discounted. I am not a stock broker, but when asked what stocks to buy, I suggest that people look at the products they purchase on a regular basis. If you are a returning customer, aren't there other returning customers? When investing, start small. Add shares slowly and build your portfolio. Steer clear of day trading, as it is tantamount to gambling.

When you approach investing, use dollar cost averaging: Invest a fixed dollar amount at the same time every month, no matter what's happening in the financial markets. That way, you ensure that you buy more shares when prices are low and fewer shares when prices are high, thereby lowering the average cost per share. Dollar cost averaging doesn't mean that you can't lose money. But because no one can pinpoint the moment a market will hit bottom or top out, investing a set amount at regular intervals makes it more likely that you'll come out ahead in the long run.

Military Money Management

As a proud Air Force brat who traveled much of the world before high school, I hold a special place in my heart for those members of our military who make great sacrifices for our country with their service while building careers and growing families.

An active war still rages in Afghanistan, and thousands and thousands of men and women are deployed – some on their fourth or fifth tour of duty. These long stretches of time away from home are not only emotionally taxing but can also be financially trying.

In Iraq, the war is over, and we will celebrate the troops' return. But they are coming home to a different battle: an unemployment rate of 9% and a scarcity of jobs. Military families' money needs and mind-set are often compromised when they are no longer serving because while on active duty, expenses are predictable and relatively low due to base housing and discounts available at the commissary and base exchange.

When it comes to money management, military families – especially young couples – are often faced with unique circumstances, including frequent relocations. Repeated moves have the potential of compromising one's money. Military families need to know concrete ways to prepare financially for a transitional lifestyle.

I remember clearly and fondly the way my parents orchestrated continuity in our lives. While Dad was reporting for duty, Mom was making yet another location a home. It was Mom who explained the customs, the history and the *money* of whatever country in which we were living.

The lessons I learned as an Air Force kid provided the foundation for me to accept and embrace the cultures, nuances, needs and disciplines of the world's people. Those lessons also helped me know early on the importance of self-reliance and personal discipline. Both of these traits form the basis with which I speak about personal money and the ability to make it, spend it, save it, invest it and manage it.

Military families have special needs when it comes to creating financial well-being and stability while *in* the military and *fresh out* of the service. There are scams, bad habits, new laws and the sobering reality that a service member could die – in which event the surviving family would receive substantial government benefits. The knowledge that's needed to manage those benefits and preserve a state of financial well-being is a necessary and important goal.

In 2003, President George W. Bush signed the Service Members Freedom Civil Relief Act, a revision of the Soldiers and Sailors Civil Relief Act. This legislation was created to help ease the economic and legal burdens on military personnel who were called to active duty status in Operation Iraqi Freedom. Most military families don't know that it provides specific provisions regarding evictions, lease terminations, repossessions, mortgage foreclosures and storage-lien foreclosures. As thousands of military families lose their homes or face bankruptcy, they need to know what their unique rights are if a family member is serving in a war zone.

It's important for military personnel and military family members to educate themselves about managing their personal money. First Lady Michelle Obama has made military families one of her special interests. "Service doesn't end with the person wearing the uniform; the war doesn't end when a soldier returns home. Military family members have their own special courage and strength," the First Lady said to a crowd of service men and women at Fort Bragg in March 2009.

Our patriots make great sacrifices for the future of the United States. In turn, they should apply that same dynamic energy when preparing for their respective financial futures.

The Change Makers

We are all works in progress. I noted that I'm not a stock broker or certified financial advisor but rather a financial literacy expert. What I bring to the work I do regarding personal money management came in part from personal experiences, including my divorce.

In 1995, while working in New York, longtime CNN senior manager Lou Dobbs asked to meet with me regarding an on-air position. Now, most people do not turn down a meeting with Lou Dobbs. But I did. I wasn't sure I wanted to make a career change. We laugh about that now, but at the time, he was a bit insulted. After his third request I said yes. Lou had been with CNN since it launched in 1980. He was the network's chief economics correspondent as well as the host of the popular business news program *Moneyline*. He was CNN's executive vice president and a member of the company's executive committee. He later founded CNNfn (CNN Financial News), serving as its president and anchoring the on-air television program *Business Unusual*, which examined business creativity and leadership.

Lou saw in me someone different than the typical Wharton Business School graduate or expert number-cruncher. He had followed my career, watched the different stories I covered in and around New York, and recognized that I had a consistent approach to dealing with issues that, paraphrasing his words, spoke to the everyday American.

There is a softer side to Lou than most people can glean from his career on television or from listening to his successful radio show. Though our political points of view were very different, he saw something in me he considered an asset for his new network: my ability to have what he called "living-room conversations" with viewers. He gave me an amazing, global platform at CNN. For this opportunity, and our friendship that continues, I will always be grateful.

When you are younger and just starting out, it's important to recognize when opportunity knocks, especially one that involves your career. Sir Isaac Newton said of his own accomplishments, "If I have seen a little further it is by standing on the shoulders of giants." All of us have our giants. Throughout the course of my life I have found inspiration from numerous people that made my life (in certain respects) easier. One such person is Madam C.J. Walker.

A daughter of former slaves, she was born Sarah Breedlove on December 23, 1867, on a Delta, Louisiana, plantation. Orphaned at age 7, she and her sister made ends meet by working long days in cotton fields.

In her late 20s, she began to suffer from a scalp ailment, causing her to lose most of her hair. Devastated, she experimented with countless homemade remedies and store-bought products, including those made by famed African American entrepreneur Annie Malone. In 1905, Sarah took a job as a sales agent with Malone's company. While she taught herself the business, she met and married her third husband, Charles Joseph Walker, a St. Louis newspaperman.

After changing her name to "Madam" C.J. Walker, she founded her own business and began selling Madam Walker's Wonderful Hair Grower, a scalp-conditioning and healing formula. The Madam said the remedy was revealed to her in a dream. She worked and saved, and educated herself, while bettering the life of her only daughter, Lelia (later known as A'Lelia Walker). In time, Madame Walker became the first African American millionaire, and today she is lauded as one of the 20th century's most successful, self-made female entrepreneurs.

Her accomplishments were far-reaching: Among other things, she opened Lelia College to train Walker "hair culturists"; contributed $1,000 to the building fund of the "colored" YMCA in Indianapolis; organized the first national meetings of businesswomen in the country; and joined a group of Harlem leaders who visited the White House to present a petition advocating for federal anti-lynching legislation, a cause supported by the NAACP (to which she donated $5,000).

She had a tough life from the start, but Madam Walker's life story is a celebration of tenacity, hard work, wit and perseverance. In 1912, at the National Negro Business League Convention, she said, "I am a woman who came from the cotton fields of the South. From there I was promoted to the washtub. From there I was promoted to the cook kitchen. And from there I promoted myself into the business of manufacturing hair goods and preparations. I have built my own factory on my own ground."

Right now, times are tough, money is tight and opportunities are often few and far between. Don't let those circumstances get you down. Think about Madam Walker's journey. If you grab hold of your finances and future goals, you, too, can persevere.

Spend Wisely, Save Wildly

I often speak to audiences of young women who are looking for tools to ensure a secure financial future. I tell them to "spend wisely and save wildly." This needs to be their mind-set.

Val-uable Money Tip:
Spend wisely and save wildly.

Not too long ago I spoke to a group of young women at the YWCA, the oldest and largest multicultural women's organization in the world. The gathering of several hundred started at 8 a.m. on a Saturday morning. To my surprise and delight, it was a full house. After my keynote address, a group gathered to ask questions. I so enjoy this aspect, meeting and talking with members of my audience one-on-one.

One woman in her late 20s waited patiently as others asked various questions. I saw tremendous strain in her face. Tears were welling in her eyes. When it was her time to speak, her voice was shaky. I reached out to her to assure her that whatever she needed to say was okay and that I'd help however I could. "I'm a *violent* saver," she blurted. Tears ran down her cheeks. She explained that her friends teased her because she always saved, and they claimed she didn't ever have "fun" because she never spent money. I told her that she was allowing them to place a negative connotation on her approach to saving. Then I told her to stop thinking of her commitment to saving money as a bad thing. She wasn't a *violent* saver; she was a *voracious* saver. Words can change attitudes. Attitudes can change habits. Changing habits can result in change(s) which can amount to major financial gains. She exhaled immediately and then actually smiled. I suggested that she deserved to reward herself every once in a while by setting aside a small amount of money regularly to have some of that "fun" her friends claimed she was missing.

In order to "get an authentic financial life," I suggest some or all of the following:

- Deliberately think about and determine your collective knowledge about money.

- Know that you don't need to make changes all at once.

- Determine your risk tolerance.

- Do aggressive planning.

- Continually educate yourself.

- Inform and assist elder family members.

- Remember that life changes are always good reassessment moments.

- Get informed and find a financial advisor.

- Be aware of inheritance issues.

- Remember philanthropy.

- Don't just have a financial résumé, have financial foresight.

Val-uable Money Tip:
Don't just have a financial résumé, have financial foresight.

As 20-somethings enter their 30s, a set of new issues is presented. If you haven't saved for retirement until this point, obviously there is still time. But don't underestimate the importance of getting a retirement fund started. According to a report from McKinsey & Co., Americans aren't saving enough for retirement, and a large percentage won't have enough assets and income to maintain their lifestyle in retirement. The average American household will have only 63 percent of the income needed.

The Melbourne Mercer Global Pension Index released a report measuring 11 leading countries based on the adequacy, sustainability and integrity of their public and private pension systems. The Netherlands received the highest ranking, followed by Australia, Sweden, Canada, the United Kingdom and the United States. Chile was number seven on the list, followed by Singapore, Germany, China and Japan.

What does this mean? Our new global economy demands that we keep in step with other countries. So if the company you are working for has a 401(k) plan with a matching contribution, take advantage of it immediately! For most Americans, their retirement goal is to have a million dollars saved. While a million dollars 25 years from today won't be worth as much as a million dollars today, it is a goal most people hope to achieve.

The fourth decade of life – ages 30 through 39 – is also a time when people start to pay attention to their health. This could include exercise and eating healthier. The same approach should be taken relating to money, says Dr. Wade. "You want to cultivate a relationship with money. Financial wellness is as important as physical wellness. Many people," she says, "cleanse, feed, nurture, exercise and maintain their bodies. But we don't do that with money."

As we consider saving for retirement, we should

look to our respective futures by respecting our past. There will always be times of economic uncertainty – that is the nature of the market. It is your approach to your finances that can better position you regardless of uncontrollable circumstances.

I continually draw strength from Madam C.J. Walker's journey. She overcame tremendous obstacles and hurdles. There is a great lesson in one of her mantras, a directive that should be embraced: "I got my start by giving myself a start." So can you. *It's your money so take it personally*®.

Chapter 7

Elder Bucks

"What material success does is provide you with the ability to concentrate on other things that really matter. And that is being able to make a difference, not only in your own life, but in other people's lives." — Oprah Winfrey

Mortality is an issue that significantly impacts a person's relationship to money and influences the way in which finances are managed. Depending where the life lens is pointed, a different picture will take shape. For young couples starting out, the idea is to find enough physical space to accommodate the family they plan to have. The unfortunate reality is that all too often there is not enough money to afford what's desired. Conversely, older couples usually have the required funds but no longer need the larger space money could buy.

As I write, my husband and I are continuing the process of sorting through the contents and memories of the home we left in Arizona as we settle back into life in the Bay Area. We left a big house in the desert that had rooms that went unused. So here we are in our early 60s. We can afford the space but no longer have use for it. When I was in my 30s with two young children, the kind of space that we just left would have been gloriously ideal.

Down-sizing versus Right-sizing

My husband and I are at the age when the concept of downsizing should be tantalizing and represent yet another rite of passage. But downsizing sounds pejorative to many baby boomers who spent a lifetime acquiring all the "stuff" that represented accomplishment and success. So don't think downsizing. Instead, think "right-sizing" – the act of consciously deciding what the environment in which you now choose to live should look like. As you go through this cathartic process, you'll begin to recognize the items that are important – the ones that you hold dear and embody memories.

These are assets that have emotional value as well. It may be jewelry or a family heirloom piece of furniture, but you know it is time to pass them on to children, grandchildren or close friends. This is a transformative process.

During our recent relocation, for example, I gave the last two of 12 family photo albums to my youngest daughter, Ciara. I was once the keeper of the family history, but that baton has been passed to her. Growing up, Ciara was always intrigued with watching the meticulous creation of the albums and showed the greatest inclination for preserving them.

These transitions are best negotiated when older family members are healthy and yet at a point in life where they are aware of the magnitude of the change that will eventually transpire.

This transformative process, and all the moving parts, awakens my golfer's mind. It's not unusual to hit a good shot, follow the flight of the ball but then lose sight of where it actually comes to rest. This happens particularly in autumn, when balls can get lost in the swirling, beautifully colored leaves that gather on many golf courses at that time of year. Often, the best way to find the ball is to drive past where you think it landed and backtrack, because it is easier to look over ground you have already covered. When the older generation begins to look for their "ball" or where they are in life right now, the view is obscured by "leaves," or memories of the life they lived. At this point it's important to understand that more life has *been* lived than there is life to *be* lived.

While elders can emotionally accommodate this reality, it is often a difficult one for their adult children to acknowledge and embrace. Many are part of what's called the Sandwich Generation – middle-aged people who often are (or will be) providing physical and financial assistance simultaneously (either by necessity or choice) for both their children and their aging parents. The adult child often is unwilling to acknowledge the potential possibility of their parent becoming ill or incapable of making sound decisions. This is why discussing elder money-management issues while parents are healthy and otherwise capable of managing their finances will help everyone focus on where the "ball" lands (new life circumstances) and what's needed when it's found (implementing the agreed-to plan).

It is at this time that adult children and parents should enter into a collaborative effort toward realistic and thoughtful asset and money-management practices. While my husband and I are thankfully healthy, we understand that it takes just one issue – one fall, one slip or one illness – to create catastrophic differences in our lives and in the lives of our family members.

These necessary "what if" conversations are almost always initially uncomfortable and awkward. Similar to what I tell couples when they are first married, I tell to adult children: You can talk about money needs and plans now, or you can struggle to figure out what your parents' wishes would have been later, in the midst of a crisis.

How to be a Parenting Child: A laundry list

When adult children approach their elders on money-management issues, they should keep the following points in mind:

- **Treat your parents with respect:** While old age can be a rewarding time, it's also often a time of loss of loved ones, loss of health and loss of independence, so reassure your parents that you will be there for them as they age.

- **Explain the purpose of your conversation:** Tell them you want to be able to do the right things for them as they age based on what you *know* they want.

- **Use good communication skills:** It's more effective if you offer options rather than advice. Express concerns, listen, don't be afraid of silence; use open-ended questions that foster discussion rather than ones answered with "yes" or "no."

- **Include other family members:** Get all the issues on the table, and gather support from siblings and other relatives.

- **Understand your parents' need to control their own lives:** Remember that they have a right to make their own decisions even if, at some point, you may need to balance their independence with their safety.

- **Agree to disagree:** Don't try to bully your way through. Their wishes should prevail unless their health or safety is in question.

- **Ask about records and documentation:** Know where your parents' insurance policies, wills, health care proxies, living wills, trust documents, tax returns, and investment and banking records are located. Start this discussion by letting them know you are updating and putting your important documents in place and want to know where they keep their papers and whom you should contact in case they're incapacitated.

- **Provide information:** Be a resource for information for your parents. They may need to know about the legal and financial options available to them, so provide materials for them to read and look for opportunities to talk with them about the information.

- **Re-evaluate if things aren't working well:** The best approach is always to be willing to assess why things aren't going well. You might need to suggest that your parents talk to a third party, such as a geriatric care manager or financial planner.

Having Your *Aha* Moment

The relocation that my husband and I went through will likely be one of our last. We understand and are at peace knowing that though modern science and medicine have increased longevity, the majority of life is behind us. This doesn't mean that we are looking toward the future grimly. It's quite the opposite. We are happy to be in control of the decisions that have been made.

In the process of packing, I physically touched so

many memories. The pictures and various mementos gave me such pause. Experts say it is usually better to reflect on memories when unpacking rather than when packing. With this tip in mind, I still found myself taking more time than I should have in fond trips down memory lane. In doing so, I had an *aha* moment. I think it was a slow-building epiphany. I realized, or admitted to myself for the first time, that I'm not an entrepreneur; I am an *intra*preneur.

I often discuss this concept with my audiences. To me, an entrepreneur is a person excited about *every* single aspect of what's required to do what it is they do – from back-office management to product development to sales. I quickly came to understand that I, on the other hand, am a specialist; I know what my skill sets are and how much I strongly enjoy exploring and using them in a 360-degree way.

As a television journalist and anchor, when I look into the camera lens, I don't see millions of people; my frame of mind has long been that I connect with one set of eyes through the lens. I feel we are all integral pieces of a puzzle that makes up a larger, cohesive image. So it was during this process of realizing that I'm an *intra-* rather than *entre*preneur that I "looked into my own eyes" to determine where I was and where I wanted to go.

Since leaving my anchor position at CNN, I have reflected on my thoughts of the future. I began referring to the next phase of my working life as my "encore career," and I have given very specific attention to clearly embracing the benefits of this new frame of mind. I remembered a book I had read called *Encore: Work That Matters in the Second Half of Life,* by San Francisco author Marc Freedman. The message resonates for me in this still-trying-to-recover-from-the-recession environment. Money and the rules of accessing it have changed, as have the retirement plans of many. You can't follow the same model from the past. In order to survive, you have to adapt. That's why it's imperative to find work that is meaningful and rewarding in the second phase of life.

Freedman wrote, "Faced with the practical necessity of extended working lives, boomers have made it a virtue, getting busy on their next chapters, second acts, or Careers 2.0. Some of the ills that seemed intractable at the beginning of the 21st century are fading, and others that appeared only to be worsening have made a 180-degree turn – all thanks to boomer labor power, now known as the 'experience dividend.'"

There Are Rules For A Reason

For many boomers, and those even older, it is

imperative to have structure in your day-to-day-life. It helps you feel relevant. Obsolescence can absolutely become a factor as people enter their mid-50s to early 60s. Again, we have lived more of our life than we probably have left. Again, I don't mean to sound negative. I'm being practical. I came across an article in the *Washington Post* (March 2010) that stated the average life expectancy was 80.7 years for women and 75.4 years for men.

Financial advisors will often suggest that elder individuals and couples retire in or around a college town. I absolutely agree. Youthful pursuits, whether social, academic or cultural, invigorate older minds. And for the younger generation, having elders in the community is a positive experience, too. Over 500 colleges and universities offer classes geared toward senior citizens – a growing trend in academia.

Urban centers can serve the same purpose for elders. In fact, in addition to the family ties we have in the San Francisco/Oakland/San Jose area, the opportunities and amenities afforded by the location made it a great choice for us. Most metropolitan areas have excellent services in place for seniors, as well as personal enrichment programs, such as the Bernard Osher Foundation's Lifelong Learning Institutes (OLLI). The more than 100 OLLI programs nationwide help institutions of higher education to develop and strengthen intellectually stimulating, noncredit courses specifically designed for students over 50 years of age. Emphasis is placed on learning for the joy of learning as well as keeping in touch with the world at large.

As I was packing my home office for our move, I came across a picture of a dear friend, Gertrude Landau, who died a few years ago at the age of 95. She graduated from City University of New York's Hunter College in 1931 and holds the unique distinction of being the founder of the world's first senior citizens' center in the Bronx (1943). She never married and was an only child. Her entire adult professional life was dedicated to senior assistance and health care. I met her while doing a series of reports on senior issues. Gertrude was living in the Manhattan apartment she'd called home for nearly 40 years. While I was interviewing her about the importance of senior centers, she told me that "women marry their husbands for better or worse, but not for lunch." Over the course of her life and career, she continually placed value on bringing men and women out of the house and into social situations as a way to strengthen their spirit and the community at large.

Gertrude also told me that "old age isn't for sissies." This wasn't an off-the-cuff remark; she meant it. Her statement underscores my position that you need to push for open communication between generations. Avoiding this topic will not make money-management issues easier; it will make them more difficult. It is not always going to be easy, but it can be accomplished in a loving, logical way.

"There are just as many kinds of old age as there are old people," said Ms. Landau, explaining that it was a mistake to regard old age as a universal experience similar to infancy. "We all slow down, but we all slow down in different ways." As in all of its stages, she added, life continued to be defined by relationships and the sense of achievement. But in old age, relationships are often lost or strained, and the possibilities for achievement tend to decline.

As I packed my photo of Gertrude, and took notes for the writing of this chapter, I was reminded of another story I had covered in the late 1980s. It spoke to the importance of caring for our elders, something all too often overlooked in our society. The Cambridge, Massachusetts – based shoe company Stride Rite opened the nation's first on-site child-care program for employees and community members in 1971. Building on that model, in 1990 it made one of its two child-care centers into an intergenerational care center for its workers' children and elder dependents.

The Bond Between Generations — A Balancing Act

There are more than 35 million people in the United States over the age of 65. The number is expected to reach 55 million by the year 2020. As a result, there is an increased need for programs that support our aging population. Intergenerational day care is one such program designed to offer daily care and support to older adults and young children. Stride Rite is not alone in facilitating this concept.

ONEgeneration, in Van Nuys, California, and My Second Home, in Mt. Kisco, New York, mix older adults and preschool children into one day-care environment. The goal is to encourage their interaction – a key component for which these shared-site facilities are specifically designed – to develop a bond between generations.

As part of the first generation of full-time working women and mothers, I was intrigued by the concept of an intergenerational day-care center because I was reminded of my maternal Grandmother "Mudd" and the time I spent with her. She even moved to England to live with us during my dad's tour of duty there. So for me, I just assumed when I was growing up that kids and elders always played together and spent time together.

Intergenerational day care is a forward-thinking, logical and comfortable way for industry to get the most out of its workforce. I believe in the cultural importance of including elders in the process of teaching upcoming generations.

When my parents retired from Air Force life to California, they did so comfortably. They purchased an RV and traveled often throughout the country, but particularly the Southwest. They enjoyed the many wonders it offered and often talked about the beauty of New Mexico.

I was always in regular contact with my parents and pretty much knew their daily activities. Yet somehow during one particular six-week period my parents never mentioned that they were house hunting. They were just "on the road again." When they finally returned home, they called and declared, "Guess what? We bought a house!" I replied, "Great! In Santa Fe or Albuquerque?" They responded, "Las Vegas." I was stunned.

My parents explained that they had spent time there and enjoyed it, and they had decided it was the best place for them. Three months later, my husband's parents made the same announcement. Both sets of elders noted that, for one thing, food was cheaper because the casinos offered inexpensive, high-quality buffets. My parents also noted that Las Vegas had become a family vacation destination and that it was the fastest growing city in the nation. In addition, Nellis Air Force Base was located there, which afforded them the benefits of the discounted prices at the base commissary and exchange store. My parents had made a smart choice based on good reasons. But I wasn't involved in the decision.

At the time, I was living in New York, my daughters were in the Bay Area, and my husband and I had a vacation home in Tucson. Now my parents were in Las Vegas. As you get older, you often want to consolidate the things that are important to you, and that includes being in proximity to your parents and the rest of your family. Getting from point A to point B takes so much effort and orchestration; travel becomes daunting. And as we age, what was once commonplace or an everyday activity grows more difficult. Of the many factors that fall under the umbrella of asset management, be sure to include dealing with the physical and emotional limitations of elders as they continue to age. But also be mindful of the limitations of their care-giving, middle-aged adult children.

A great benefit of being a reporter is that you have never-ending continuing education. When I bought our family vacation home in Tucson, in Pima County, Arizona, I recall telling my friends how comfortable I was there. The unobstructed view of stars and constellations in the desert skies, the beauty and varieties of cacti – I really felt at *home.* I was anchoring at CNN at the time and did a story on a new genealogy company in Washington, D.C., called African Ancestry, which traced ancestral history by using DNA samples. While I knew of my maternal Native American roots, I was absolutely shocked to learn that my blood line ran to the Pima Indians, who have inhabited southern Arizona for more than 2,000 years.

It was exploring Spaniards who first encountered this tribe in the 1600s. They named the tribe Pima. Archaeological digs uncovered evidence that the Pima Indians were master weavers and farmers who established a sophisticated system of irrigation that made the desert fruitful with wheat, beans, squash and cotton. The women of the community made exquisite baskets so intricately woven that they were watertight.

The idea of watertight baskets spoke to me on many levels. Water is a life force, not unlike money. Taking progressive, proactive asset-management steps with elders will help to ensure that the *basket* containing their finances is secure and tight.

Identifying your support team

It is no easy task to weave such a basket. While speaking with my good friend Mary Beth Franklin, a senior editor at *Kiplinger's Personal Finance* magazine and editor of its annual *Retirement Planning Guide,* we discussed the rather tough position that many boomers are in as they care for their children as well as their parents and still have to determine when or if they will be able to retire as planned.

"Many older workers in their 50s and 60s are in a precarious position. For some, the only option is to work longer," says Franklin. "Working longer is a powerful strategy for several reasons: It allows you more time to save; gives your investments more time to recover; decreases the number of years you need to rely on those savings; and boosts your Social Security benefits, which are worth more the longer you wait to claim them, up to age 70."

As we get older, it is important to limit potential damages to an investment portfolio. Elders must be sure they are working with an experienced accountant or other financial specialist who will help them figure out in what order they should use their retirement money and why. (For example, there are tax implications to consider when liquidating portfolios.)

Every person has different needs, so every person should establish new goals and select a financial advisor who will help bring those goals to fruition. What is the biggest fear for elders? Outliving their money. Even those who saved judiciously might now, thanks to modern medicine, live longer than expected and therefore require more money in retirement.

Parents almost always are looking at ways to take care of their children and grandchildren, but they *must* put their own financial needs first. The overwhelming majority of people in their 60s and 70s have to be careful about giving money as gifts. Unless you are independently wealthy, you can't afford to give money away because you are not actively making money. My mantra for elders is: Find ways to save.

Val-uable Money Tip:
Elders must find ways to save.

Finding ways to save will contribute to an elder's

retirement account. Savings should be looked at as income. Spending should be deliberate. Go back to basics: Is it a *need* or a *want*? Reward yourself when you deserve to be rewarded. But moderation and foresight are required.

Adult children who are caring for elders can reinforce sound money-management strategies by having a certified financial specialist in the mix. With over 500 amendments made to tax laws each year, it makes sense to consult a professional.

Elders who are of healthy mind and body but do not have children or other family members to assist them in these decisions should reach out to a recommended certified financial planner in the community. You need someone in your life who will provide you with guidance. There is simply no way for most people over the age of 60 to fully understand how each tax law applies to his or her assets.

Be Your Own Genie So Your Wishes Are Granted

Everyone who is 18 or older should have a will in place. For elders, it is important to revisit your will to make sure your beneficiary designations are accurate. Perhaps as important, make sure that your family knows you have a will, where it is *and what is in it*. Wills are not meant to be surprises, and I don't believe surprising people after you're gone is a good idea. If you made out your will while you were of sound mind, in good health and of benevolent spirit, why not share the information with those who have been designated to receive your assets?

Wills can always be changed. You might hear about fights between parents and children that result in a child losing his or her inheritance. There will always be extremes in life, no matter the issue. It is important not to focus on the exception to the rule but the rule itself, which is always to have your will in order.

When money-management issues with elders are expertly navigated, relationships often grow in new, positive directions. The American dream is to work hard throughout your life and create a loving home full of memories. This is perhaps the greatest definition of success and a reality we all wish to attain.

Oprah Winfrey was right when she said that material success provides us the opportunity to concentrate on those things that really matter so that we can make a difference in other people's lives. If all you want to do is gather possessions, eventually they will possess you. While we all have tribulations in life, it's what we do when faced with them that matters. In order to do well for yourself, you must also do good to others.

It's Your Money So Take It Personally

Chapter 8

Suddenly Single

"We have become 99 percent money mad.
The method of living at home modestly and within
our income, laying a little by [aside] systematically
for the proverbial rainy day which is due to come,
can almost be listed among the lost arts."
— *George Washington Carver*

Whether married, in a partnership or in a committed relationship, many people believe that being a couple is the best way to go through life. So there is perhaps nothing more emotionally devastating than losing the beloved partner with whom you shared a wonderful life.

Whenever you are in the midst of an emotional situation and you make a decision regarding money, your choices will likely be different than choices made when you're not under duress. Becoming suddenly single can be as result of a divorce or being widowed. But sometimes being single is a decision made by choice. After all, a marriage or committed relationship is not for everyone.

When it comes to widowhood, my advice is that assets that are inherited should be placed in a safe, secure account where they can earn interest. This gives you the immediate, initial time to grieve. The length of time needed to come to grips with a loss emotionally will be different for everyone, but roughly it takes about one year. Then you are better able to decide what it is you want to do with the inheritance.

Saying Goodbye

My most recent experience with being suddenly single was when my parents died. While most of the time this situation applies to spouses and partners, as I mentioned earlier, I was alone to deal with my parents' estates when they died. In terms of my original nuclear family, I was suddenly single.

After my mother died, and my father remained

seriously ill, I had extreme difficulty concentrating and coping with her loss while making sure my father was cared for and looked after. My father died six months after my mother, just a few days before Christmas. It was a devastating and emotionally demanding period of my life.

I thought I had given myself enough time to grieve. It was the first of February. My parents' ashes finally had been buried at Arlington National Cemetery (the date and time of burial are selected and assigned by Arlington; it was a month and a few days after my dad's death). I decided to begin addressing issues related to their estates. I always advise people to make a call regarding settling an estate or other financial situations that are part of the "business of death and dying" only when you are having a good day, because if you're in a fragile state of mind, you may be unknowingly bullied.

I thought I was in a good frame of mind. I called the Social Security Administration. I was on the phone for much of the day being referred from one clerk or representative to another. Finally, I found myself on the line with an abrupt woman. She had a terse tone. My parents raised me to be a polite person and despite this woman's crassness, I calmly introduced myself and explained that I was calling as a result of my parents' deaths. I barely finished my sentence when she gruffly said, "What was the day of her death?" I provided the date. I told the woman that I lost my father six months later. "I need more information on your mother," she returned with no emotion. I felt myself beginning to crumble. According to her records, she told me, my father predeceased my mother. *What?* They were wrong, but she wouldn't listen to reason. She was steadfast in telling me the order of my parents' deaths, despite me telling her the truth. "Call us back when you have your facts straight," she said before hanging up the phone. I sobbed uncontrollably. I *knew* when my parents died. The Social Security Administration records were wrong. I did not do anything further regarding my parents' estates. I was immobilized.

If you are the surviving family member, be good to yourself by taking the time to heal and become resolute. Then when the time comes to deal with the business of death, you are at your strongest and people can't bully you into a frame of mind to make decisions that aren't necessarily going to be beneficial in the long run.

A bit more than a week passed before I felt strong enough to try and correct the Social Security Administration's records. Then I put on my journalist cap and began researching all the necessary steps I had to take to address my parents' documents and accounts with Social Security, insurance and the military.

A major concern was figuring out how to settle their insurance bills, which were huge. My parents had three policies. I knew from my disconcerting experiences with the Social Security Administration that I would not be able to expertly navigate the settlement of three insurance plans, some of which had overlapping clauses and coverage. I began to see a difficult puzzle emerge, and at stake was hundreds of thousands of dollars in medical bills and claims relating to my parents shared estate.

Identifying Your Support Team

Instead of getting overwhelmed, I hired a geriatric care specialist. I had originally engaged Lyndi Anderson when my parents were still alive. I was living in New York. I wanted someone that was within minutes of them geographically who could deal with any and all issues relating to their health care. Lyndi's practice was in Tucson, and she lived just blocks away from my mom and dad's retirement community. While I visited frequently, I simply could not continue flying back and forth every time there was a financial issue or health concern. She was my elder care specialist and elder care angel.

$\approx$

Valuable Money Tip:
To locate a geriatric care specialist in your community, visit <u>www.caremanager.org</u>.

$\approx$

My elderly parents and their middle-aged, baby-boomer daughter were the mutual beneficiaries of this decision. As a result of this experience, I'm a proponent and advocate for using the services of geriatric care specialists. These professionals are dedicated to providing quality of life to elders. Before my mother died, she was stricken with *Alzheimer's* disease. Regardless of their individual health issues, it was imperative that my parents stayed together. I knew that their end-of-life well-being depended on that. Lyndi was able to secure a room for my mother at a leading local Alzheimer's facility. On top of that, she was able to negotiate terms so that my father could move in too! He was the only resident who didn't have a form of dementia, so the staff thoroughly enjoyed his company. He received great care and everyone loved talking with him. My mother was getting the care she needed, and my father got his wish to be by her side.

It was in the weeks after the horrible Social Security call that I found myself reflecting on Lyndi and the dignity she provided my parents as they entered their last phase of life – and the peace of mind she provided me, the long-distance, adult-child caregiver.

I realized that I needed her assistance again to manage the medical bills and gave her a call. She took care of all the insurance matters as well as those remaining issues with Social Security. That is how I returned to solid footing. I was able to handle certain aspects of the estate settlement, but I felt confident passing other responsibilities to a geriatric care professional (who will charge approximately $35 and up per hour).

On Lyndi's recommendation, I also consulted an elder care attorney, a decision which was put in motion before my parents' deaths. This decision should be discussed by spouses, partners, guardians or care givers while elders are of sound mind and body so that there are no surprises down the road as medical conditions dictate potentially serious and emotional decisions, such as guardianship. You need an experienced, well-versed advocate who will fight for your concerns and your parents' needs.

When a loved one dies, regardless of age, you fall into a mentality that fits your emotional state.

You think, *Shouldn't the world stop for a moment and acknowledge the absence of this person?* It's as if you want an extended moment of silence that lasts for however long your grieving period is. But we know that doesn't happen.

In my experience, hiring a geriatric care specialist and an elder law attorney provides the opportunity for you to take a deep breath and find solace during dark, difficult days. This approach also allows you to begin the process of making smart money-management decisions regarding bequeathed assets.

End-of-Life Checklist

What to have on hand:
- Name of accountant, address and phone number.

- Bank and/or credit union accounts with institution name, account numbers and information on any safe deposit boxes.

- List of pension plans, life insurance policies and real estate along with policy numbers and contact information.

- Stockbroker's name, address and phone number.

- Names of beneficiaries, their contact

information and policies assigned.

- All deeds, stock certificates, investment and retirement accounts.

What you'll need to do:
- Review all insurance policies and beneficiary designations for them.

- Do a net worth statement.

- Consult a certified financial planner.

- Sign a living will or a living trust.

- Prepare and execute advance directives (a living will and medical power of attorney) for your state.

- Keep these documents in an accessible place.

- Photocopy originals and give copies to doctors, family, clergy and others who will be involved in your end-of-life care/needs.

- Create a financial inventory regarding possessions you want to go to whom upon your death.

- Create a "bucket list" of any goals you want to accomplish and what they will cost.

Becoming suddenly single is overwhelming

regardless of the situation. Prepare by practicing the mind-over-money basics of protecting your assets, not making rash decisions with your inheritance and providing yourself the necessary time to heal emotionally.

Divorce

To say divorce is complicated would be an understatement. I hope that those people who face divorce will have had their own independent, personal financial life in place consistently and deliberately throughout their marriage. This means they are better prepared if and when such an event happens. And if you *don't* have your own financial identity and you're reading this (even if you are happily married), I hope you will know that it is never too late – but urgently important – to get one.

Divorce rarely results from "Honey, I'm home. Guess what? I'm not happy. I want a divorce." A divorce is usually a long time coming, with telltale signs. Once you see the first sign of distress, you should make sure your financial life is as sound as it can be, because that will be the foundation from which you will need to start anew.

Look for any signs that your relationship is in trouble. If you discover a problem, the most beneficial approach you can take is to understand that despite being in the midst of a relationship that is falling apart, you know how much money you have, where it is, and how you can access it, grow it, manage it and make it work for you. If you haven't embraced this mantra before, now more than ever is the time to commit to it: *It's your money so take it personally*®.

If your marriage started with the philosophy of "what's mine is yours and what's yours is mine" and everything is commingled, you will run into problems if the marriage deconstructs. Taking individual financial measures, such as purchasing real estate independently, will place you individually in a secure position while benefiting the family unit as a whole.

Edward Tanenbaum, a tax and estate planning attorney and partner in the New York office of Alston and Bird LLP, told me, "If a couple is facing a divorce, and they have not entered into a prenuptial agreement, each spouse may want to take steps to do a new will that protects their intended beneficiaries after the divorce. Should one spouse pass away before the divorce is finalized, the surviving spouse may still have a claim to a portion of the deceased spouse's estate."

I've said it before and will say it again: I am a

romantic. It is my hope that marriages, partnerships and relationships will go on wonderfully forever. But I am also a realist. You have to love yourself as much or more than your partner.

Many couples will enter into a period of legal separation as a last-ditch effort to save the marriage. This is a tricky time because emotions are running high, and if one spouse suggests redefining financial practices it can be viewed as insensitive or threatening. Even if the marriage stays intact, recalculating financial arrangements and more openly discussing issues will provide a better second chance for a couple or partnership. Never let money conversations turn negative or sour. Rather, make your partner understand that you are being proactive with money-management practices so that whether you move forward as a couple or as individuals, it is for the better.

Val-uable Money Tip:

Whenever you experience major life changes, recalculate your relationship with your money.

When I asked Dr. Wade why people feel victimized by money, which often happens during divorce, she told me, "People don't feel in charge of their money or feel that they have any power. They can't approach money problems from a position of knowledge and therefore feel powerless."

Whenever you experience major life changes, recalculate your relationship with your money so that you have both knowledge and power. What do you need to do? Talk to a financial planner and get a handle on your money and assets. Find out your credit score and (especially if you're facing separation or divorce) make sure there are no joint accounts linked to your credit history. If there are, handle it by contacting the financial institutions in which the joint accounts reside and officially change the status. Locate all bank accounts, credit cards, insurance documents. Who has the health insurance policy? If you don't know whether the cable bill is in both of your names, find out. Don't leave any financial stone unturned.

This is when you should open the proverbial Pandora's Box and reexamine all aspects of your financial portfolio. It's a necessary accounting and purging. This is not an easy task, but whether you reunite or divorce, both individuals will have a clearer understanding of their own assets and their joint assets and be able to develop a sound money plan. And after going through this difficult process, you will realize why it is imperative that every single person have his or her own financial thumbprint.

As noted in previous chapters, when I divorced, I did so while making significant *mi$$ed-takes*. During my divorce, I had many of what I called "pity parties." There was only one invitee: me. I did this when my daughters were on sleepovers with friends and I had the house to myself. I would play music, drink a favorite beer, read and always end up having a good cry. A pity party allows you to say to yourself, *I don't deserve this. This is awful. I never planned for this to happen to me. This isn't the life I expected.*

After my pity party, before I went to sleep, I would write down the three most important things I had to do in the morning, because the pity party was over the moment I woke up. I had to start the process of building my new life.

My ex-husband was a good man and worked hard, but I was the main breadwinner, earning a much higher salary. This was the 1970s. I fully adopted the "what is mine is yours" concept. It was a time when an African American woman was often afforded more opportunities – promotions, salary increases, middle-management positions and career mentoring – than many equally qualified, hardworking African American men.

Because I was making more money, I felt that in my marriage I had to – wanted to – try to balance this issue and share everything equally. Love is complicated, and it makes you do things that you otherwise wouldn't do. I made my choices with full heart and full spirit. But these early *mi$$ed-takes* are in large part why I approach the management of personal money the way I do.

I cared about my credit score when I was first married, back when it wasn't a topic of conversation or an issue you're reminded of on television (as it is these days via catchy commercial jingles). Today, my credit score is in the top 2 percent in the country. That doesn't mean I'm a wealthy American. It simply means that I have been deliberate with my financial thumbprint and maintained everything to the point that, I concede, I'm somewhat neurotic when it comes to money management. This is a direct consequence of my divorce and the lessons I learned.

Aside from living in a community-property state and willingly commingling our assets, my ex-husband and I were left with shared debt after the divorce. Of that total debt, one poor investment alone totaled $60,000. Every month when I received that statement with both our names on it, I was reminded of the past and what was no longer. I worked hard to pay off that debt just as quickly as possible. One of the most satisfying days of my post-divorce life was when I paid that loan off and was free to live my financial life on *my* terms and only in my name.

Happily Ever After - Unmarried

There are many people who are single by choice. I respect people who make that decision, though others often judge it negatively and see it as contrary to what everybody else is doing. Similarly, I respect couples who stay together and do not get married. People may ask of a couple, "Why aren't you married?" My reaction? It's none of their business! And among couples who choose to marry and choose *not* to have children, the questions are often predictable: Is it because you are infertile or because of this or that? Oftentimes, it is none of the assumed scenarios. And it shouldn't be anyone's business or open for scrutiny. But our society unfairly deems couples without children different or somehow off the mark.

A recent Time/CNN poll found that 61 percent of single women between the ages of 18 and 49 said that they would contemplate raising a child on their own. The survey asked what women would most miss about being married. Just 4 percent said they would miss not having children.

In 2002, *Unmarried to Each Other: The Essential Guide to Living Together as an Unmarried Couple* was published. Among the unmarried author's findings: Over 5 million heterosexual couples are cohabiting in the U.S., a 200 percent increase since 1980. Many celebrities are happily unmarried, including Oprah Winfrey and Stedman Graham (25 years), Goldie Hawn and Kurt Russell (26 years), and Jessica Lange and Sam Shepard (29 years).

These statistics underscore that people have different approaches to societal conventions such as marriage and parenthood. You may agree or disagree with the swing of this pendulum, but nevertheless, it swings. So there are millions of people who choose to live together as life partners but do not marry.

There are many financial benefits to being married, but there are also benefits to not being married, including:

- Less liability. (Unmarried couples are not financially responsible for judgments against partners, such as personal lawsuits or Internal Revenue Service queries.)

- Fewer credit and debt concerns. (Unmarried couples can avoid responsibility for a partner's debts. Be careful entering into joint transactions.)

- Survivor's benefits. (By remaining single, a surviving spouse can keep the federal benefits resulting from the death of a deceased spouse. If the surviving spouse remarries, that benefit is lost.)

- Lower taxes. (While lessened over time, a marriage tax penalty still exists, which unmarried couples avoid.)

Starting Anew

After my divorce, I never thought I would marry again. I was *almost* sure of it – until I met Robert, who was first a friend. Our friendship slowly grew into a romantic relationship. I remember our paths crossing at the Montreux Jazz Festival, an annual event held each July on the banks of the beautiful shores of Lake Geneva (Switzerland). He was there with someone else. I later learned he was escorting a woman from a former relationship that had resulted in a breakup. They were giving it one more shot to see whether they could rekindle the flame. I thought they looked like a handsome couple. I didn't give it much more thought. I was there to enjoy jazz with my friends!

A few months later, mutual friends happily intervened and put us in touch. Soon after, we spent an afternoon date discussing how much we enjoyed Montreux. Our relationship slowly unfolded. Everyone else said, "You two are *such* a couple." We held steadfast that we were just very good friends. We both firmly believed then (and still do) that good friendships make for great relationships. He was also divorced and had two daughters, as did I.

As our relationship grew, our children had mixed feelings about the prospect of our marriage. We each had a daughter who wasn't keen on the idea. In any second marriage involving children there will be issues. We don't refer to ourselves as "step" anything. Robert will say, "We have four daughters." When asked how old they are, he replies that they are "33, 34, 34 and 38 this year." Immediately people look at me and say, "Oh, you had a baby and then twins a year later? Wow!"

When I'm asked how many children we have, my reply is, "His two and my two are our four," and then give their ages. His daughters have a good mother, who is actively involved in their lives and whom I respect. And I don't use the euphemism that we are a "blended family." We have managed to create a commingled family dynamic that over the years is sensitive to everyone's feelings. Just because he and I fell in love doesn't mean everyone else in our lives did, nor should they be expected to do the same.

When Robert and I approached getting married, we decided to keep our finances separate but equal. For example, we keep a notebook in the kitchen and we write down all expenditures for that month, from dry cleaning to groceries to car insurance. Whoever paid writes the amount and the date, then puts his or her initials beside it. We track the differences at the end of the month. Whoever paid less writes a check for the difference. That check goes into our shared savings account. We use that money to buy shared items, such a new flat-screen television, or we put the money toward our vacations.

This approach allows us to know our budget, what has been spent and what our discretionary funds are monthly. The last is a form of forced savings. That is the beauty of having a plan when it comes to money because you can save or use those discretionary funds more deliberately.

We don't even bank at the same bank. I did that during my first marriage – everything in one place, and in one bank. I was burned. Once bitten, twice shy. Robert and I have used these money-management practices for nearly 20 years. Do we have money issues? Absolutely. But he will readily tell people when the subject comes up that "Val's our family CFO."

There are many situations in which people will choose not to make active, aggressive financial decisions because they are waiting for something else or someone else to be the trigger, or because they don't want decisions about money to impact other things they consider valuable, such as love. As I repeatedly say, "When it comes to love and money, you can talk about it now, or fight about it later."

The kind of paralysis that comes when couples don't or won't talk the dollars and make sense of money issues can only be rectified when every single person understands that they need to have knowledge of their own financial thumbprint.

Everyone needs to be their own financial mentor so that if and when you want to pool resources for something, whether it is a marriage or a business venture, you'll make the decision from the mind-set of an informed, money-savvy individual.

A widower, a divorcee, people in the midst of a separation, or those who choose to remain single or happily unmarried have a common denominator in that they should all strive to have their respective individual financial priorities in order.

So despite where you find yourself – married, single, a partner, a significant other or some other definition that is acceptable to you – when considering your financial future, reflect on what George Washington Carver said: "[Preparing for the] proverbial rainy day which is due to come can almost be listed among the lost arts." Instead, be deliberate and commit to continually educating yourself about the art of personal money management. Again, *it's your money so take it personally*®.

Chapter 9

———ᴍ———

The Age of Un-Retirement

"You should set goals beyond your reach so you always have something to live for." — Ted Turner

The number one question I hear during conversations I have with fellow boomers at cocktail parties or on the golf course is: Can I realistically retire? The answers they give include: "No. I'm going to work longer than I thought." Or "No. I had to access retirement money sooner than I thought." Or "I'd have to take my Social Security earlier than anticipated in order to do that."

Despite your best-laid retirement plans, a recession came along and turned them upside down. So now is the time to set your new normal. Regroup and reassess your *cents*-abilities. By that I mean when you're in your 60s and beyond, your mantra should be: *Find* money to save. I'm not being a Grinch with this suggestion. Enjoy the lifestyle you can afford, but always actively save money whenever possible.

As Marc Freedman's book *Encore* states, when it comes to boomers and their realistic futures, the game has changed. "Tens of millions of baby boomers are entering a period of their lives between midlife and the onset of true old age. For most, this period will not only be a new stage of life, but also of work," noted Freedman. "I wrote this book to provide a vision of hope – not only for their own fulfillment, but for a nation where a full quarter of the population will soon be over sixty."

The message that Freedman and I share is there's hope for the approximately 76 million boomers – many of whom were getting ready to retire when this Great Recession hit. We have to reinvent ourselves by finding an encore career, which is the best way to become or remain solvent in the midst of our country's financial disarray. The indicators are everywhere. The Employee Benefit Research Group's

2010 Retirement Confidence Survey found that 69 percent of respondents said that they and/or their spouse have not saved adequately for retirement. And when it came to understanding savings goals, 46 percent reported that they hadn't calculated how much money they will need to save for a comfortable retirement.

According to a recent report released by the Population Reference Bureau, as more seniors hold on to jobs (due to falling home values and decreased stock portfolios), the workforce will increase by 11.9 million. Seniors will make up nearly one in four workers by 2016. The annual growth of retirement-destination counties in states such as Florida, Arizona and California slipped from 3.1 percent between 2000 and 2007 to 1.7 percent between 2007 and 2009.

My husband I moved from Arizona back to the San Francisco Bay Area for a number of reasons, but among them were our respective "encore" careers. I decided to leave my anchor position at CNN to focus on my encore career: financial literacy. After I made the decision, I was completely caught off-guard when the recession came along and washed away my plans. I was *planning* on transferring from earning a salary at CNN to earning an equivalent salary that I would make with keynote addresses, speeches, workshops and other financial-literacy pursuits. While I thankfully maintained a solid client roster, other opportunities began to dissipate and I had to refocus my energies.

I could have stared into the rearview mirror, looking for what should have been or what could have been. I instead opted to be positive and capitalize on those opportunities that were available. I'm not alone. This recession has forced millions to recalculate and renegotiate their futures. Welcome to the encore-career party!

The upside of an economic downturn is that the stock market resets itself about every 20 years. For those of us in our 60s, this would mean that by the time we're in our 80s, the market could be completely different. We also have to be realistic and adopt a frame of mind that takes into account the immediate future of family economics. We have to set an example and be more responsible and more passionate than ever before about making money decisions.

The Time to Act Is Now

There is nothing like a financial crisis to get everyone's attention. And no matter your age, this recession has been a wake-up call. It has provided an opportunity for boomers to have more personal and detailed conversations about money with each other and with family members.

While in theory every generation should get better at communicating about money matters, the recession forced the issue and now many families are collaborating financially to make ends meet. Over the past few years, a significant number of baby boomers lost retirement savings and, in some cases, their homes. As a result, boomers and their boomerang children (and maybe even the boomers' elderly parents) often find themselves living together again in order to survive. This collective approach hasn't been experienced in many generations, and possibly not since the Great Depression.

There are some benefits to this economic downturn. It has put a spotlight on family relations. In addition, as adult children witness the harsh impact of the recession on their boomer parents, they are beginning to focus on their own retirement savings, with greater understanding and conviction about why beginning to save for retirement in your 20s is a smart and necessary thing to do. A terrific, albeit difficult, lesson learned.

Not unlike my grandson Morgan's first money lessons about the difference between wants and needs, boomers have to go back to basics and determine their respective *needs* as opposed to *wants*. It requires a new mind-set. And because one size doesn't fit all, each person has to take personal account of their needs and how they will meet them.

I know a woman who did what she thought would guarantee security in her retirement years – she worked hard her entire life, saved and planned. Her dream was to take up sailing, touring the world by boat. As a result of the recession, she was unfortunately faced with the probability that she would not reach her dream of stopping work and traveling at the age of 60. I told her to have a pity party. I told her that pity parties have only one attendee, you, and that they are over when you wake up the next morning having written down your new goals the night before. She didn't have to give up her dream; she just needed to figure out how she was going to recalculate her approach to attaining it. Achieving it would require discipline. Her new reality is that she will likely have to work another five-plus years, but she has new goals and is prepared to meet them.

Pity-Party Checklist
- Invitation: you.

- Allow yourself the opportunity to let it all out – grieve, feel sorry for yourself and, if you need to, have a good cry.

- Determine your goals and write them down.

- Go to bed.

- Wake up and start anew with your goals in place. The pity party is over.

This is a complicated time for so many people. Some boomers have gotten so far behind on their mortgage that they owe more on the house than it's worth. I'm not going to advise them to walk away from the investment, but if they're struggling every month with a mortgage they can never get in front of again, it's like spitting in the ocean in hopes of raising the sea level. It doesn't make a difference. Instead, if you're struggling to keep up with your payments, find a good attorney for a limited (affordable) consultation to help you determine your viable options so that you can come to better understand your rights. Then, invest in finding and meeting with a certified financial planner to help you determine the best next steps and how to allocate your money to these new goals.

You need to find a person with whom you can construct an expert financial plan. Even when you have limited funds, in order to take care of your money, you often have to spend money. In the case of an out-of-control mortgage, paying for advice may very well save you money. I understand that spending money is hard to do when you don't have the money to spend, but that is why it is critical to recalculate your goals. If you're headed toward bankruptcy, for example, then educate yourself on what it entails, what it will mean to your financial thumbprint and why the decision is the best choice for you and your situation.

Par for the Course Isn't Average — It's Exceptional

This decision is like the game of golf. The worst shots are usually the ones you make when you take your eye off the ball. If you keep your head still and focus on the ball, you have a much better chance at hitting a solid shot. It's the same with money. You have to concentrate on the "ball," which might represent your mortgage or retirement accounts. The "intended shot" represents payments, investments and savings. The end goal is your ball dropping "in the cup" on the green, which represents controlling your money.

Take one swing – one money problem – at a time, with the understanding that you're trying to shoot your best game by improving incrementally, every time. There are difficult shots that require calculation: Do you need a nine iron, a putter or a hybrid (my favorite club)? Your "financial hybrid" may be a new budgeting tool and your trusty "putter" a newly hired CPA. Whatever the case, you must commit to your choice of club and then use it with confidence. Similarly, when it comes to money, if you don't have a committed plan, you will be in trouble.

Keep Your Friends Close — Keep Your Creditors Closer

You must evaluate how you got into the position you are in. Own your past actions and decisions, then act with urgency because procrastination is costly. If I have a money concern, I face it. My approach to any serious situation that I need to own up to: Be the one to tell it, tell it first and tell it all.

And when dealing with creditors, don't shoot the messenger. Make these representatives your new best friends. Be polite. Let them know that you are confident they *can* help you. Be in control and in charge of all your financial dealings this way. Anyone questioning or trying to access your records will have to be fortified with information, because you are a financially informed individual who knows your basic rights and how to protect them. Scams do exist, and the last thing you want to happen is to give personal information to the wrong person – someone who then steals your identity. This circumstance would trump your debt issue.

Val-uable Money Tip:
When confronting financial problems:
Tell it yourself, tell it first and tell it all.

In order to make good decisions when you're in financial disarray, you need to have someone with whom you can have honest, straightforward conversations – not unlike those between an expert caddy and a golf pro. The caddy (your financial expert) should be able to provide the player (you) with a metric by which you can see your target (the distance / time frame to your identified goal), know where you are in the whole scheme of your money issues (at the tee, in the middle of the fairway or just a short chip away from the green) and offer sound solutions (the best approach or course of action).

Downsizing, which I refer to as right-sizing, is a big topic among boomers: Should I? Could I? Will I? For me, the answer was yes to all three questions. When it comes to getting older, less is often more, and it is one of the greatest gifts we can give ourselves at this point in life. Look to your assets and determine what you can do without, be it real estate, automobiles or other costly possessions that require maintenance. Depending on your age, you can try to wait out the market, in the case of real estate holdings. But if you're over 60 years of age, liquidating unnecessary assets might better serve you as you approach your "recalculated" retirement years.

You Don't Have to Step in It

In the mid-1970s while working for KRON-TV Channel 4 in San Francisco, I covered Harvey Milk, an American politician who became the first openly gay man to be elected to public office in California. He won a seat on the San Francisco Board of Supervisors. Sean Penn did an impressive and precise job portraying him in the recent motion picture on his life, *Milk.*

I covered many stories about the Board of Supervisors, but the one I distinctly remember was about Supervisor Harvey Milk and his "Pooper Scooper" law. I interviewed him at Duboce Park in the city's Castro/Upper Market district, where he had a prototype scooper and staged "litter." He said, with a beaming smile, "Whoever can solve the dog-shit problem can be elected mayor of San Francisco – even president of the United States." Harvey told me that he could have just as easily held a press conference about the issue at City Hall, but it wouldn't have the required impact to effect change. He was right.

He made the front page of the paper, and his aforementioned comment led local-station newscasts that day.

So there I was with my camera crew in the park. I was walking around in my high heels. With a grin, Harvey said to me, "Watch where you step with those fabulous stilettos." Harvey always had a fun, edgy air about him. He enticed you into his space and then delivered a significant and memorable one-liner. Harvey, along with Mayor George Moscone, a close friend of mine, would later be assassinated by Dan White, a disgruntled former member of the city's board of supervisors who'd recently resigned. It was a devastating blow that cut short two political careers that will always be remembered.

My take away that afternoon in San Francisco's Duboce Park with Harvey was that sometimes you have to show people the consequences of not picking up after a dog and what it can do to your favorite pair of shoes.

All these years later, I remember this story about Harvey. As it did the day the story aired, his message provided a lesson of value. The collateral humor keeps it memorable: Sometimes you have to show people the consequences of being in certain places. When it comes to managing your money, if you're aware of where you're going and take a careful path, you don't have to step in a financial mess.

The Financial Retirement Pyramid for Baby Boomers

Boomers of different ages (the generation includes those born between 1946 and 1964) have to plan differently for retirement.

Today, one in nine Americans is a boomer. One person turns 50 every 8 seconds; that's ten thousand people a day for the next 20 years, according to Transgenerational.org, a design company that makes products for this 76 million member American demographic. The first wave of aging boomers will have reached full retirement age by New Year's Day 2012. For the next two decades, ten thousand new retirees will be added to the Social Security and Medicare rolls each day.

In the sixth decade of life (ages 50-59) you need to do with your money what you're hopefully doing with your mind and body: firming it up in general but, most important, assessing your retirement *options*. Now is the time to decide what kind of retirement lifestyle you want and plan accordingly.

Val-uable Money Tip:
Allocate 50/50 after the age of 50:
50 percent in stocks and 50 percent in bonds.

The closer you get to this thing called "retirement," the more you need to scale back on doing anything too risky with your money. Your asset allocation should be 50 percent stocks and 50 percent fixed-income securities, such as bonds. This mix lets half of your retirement savings grow in the market while providing a safety net of sorts for the other half. If, however, you're behind in your savings, you may need to be a more aggressive investor – in other words, take more risk, even in your mid-50s, in order to make up for lost time or recent losses due to the sour economy. Crunch the numbers – from Social Security, a pension and any other income sources – to determine how to best allocate your assets.

Val-uable Money Mantra:
I will make good money choices from this point forward.

It's absolutely never too late to get better informed and educated about your money. Instead of beating yourself up for the money decisions you could have, should have or would have made in years gone by, make today the first day of the rest of your improved, redirected and responsible financial life.

Val-uable Money Tip:
To calculate your assets in preparation for retirement, look for online calculators to assist you, such as the one available at www.bankrate.com/brm/news/retirement.asp.

Source: Bankrate, Inc.

Because women still, on average, live longer than men and will therefore need money for a longer period of time, it's very important to remember to actively *continue* saving for retirement. Save as much as you can, whenever you can, and be sure to track your assets more closely the closer you get to retirement.

Giving Care

At some point in our lives, nearly all of us will become a family caregiver. More than 25 percent of U.S. households are involved in some way with elder care. The MetLife Study of American Households Involved in Senior Care estimates that 30 to 40 percent of workers will assist elderly parents in the year 2020, compared with 12 percent today.

According to statistics from the United States Department of Agriculture's Personnel and Document Security Division, one-third to one-half of elder caregivers are also employed *outside* the home and sacrifice job performance, productivity, career opportunities and therefore the possibility of higher future earnings. Distracted workers aren't productive workers. Work disruptions due to employees' elder-care-giving responsibilities result in productivity losses of more than $2100 a year per employee. The Family Caregiver Alliance National Center on Caregiving says that eventually, 12 percent quit their jobs to provide elder care full-time. Be sure to ask if your employer offers an Employee Assistance Program, which will help you find related elder-care services, geriatric case managers and so forth.

Val-uable Money Tip: Recommended Elder-Care Service

*CareGuide delivers tailored health management solutions to support everyone from the healthy to the ill. Its program integrates with your other health care programs and exchanges data so that all vendors can deliver personalized care at lower costs (*www.careguide.com*).*

Many of us age 55 and older are taking care of aging parents, dealing with their end-of-life issues and what may be required of us emotionally and financially to help them. It's easy to let our *own* future money needs get sidetracked. Many parents are living longer these days, and while we're grateful for their increased longevity, it often means they're outliving their savings. It's not always easy to become elderly

– as my dear friend Gertrude Landau said, "old age isn't for sissies" – but it's also not easy to become a parenting baby-boomer adult child. You are faced with the challenge of handling your parents' financial needs as well as your own and those of your children.

Retiring

I don't believe in scare tactics. Yes, the recession has significantly altered retirement plans, but that is not to say you will not be able to enjoy your golden years. You just have to be smart about it *now*.

To this end, take a look at where you are at this point in life compared with where you thought you'd be. What better time to establish new ground rules (a new normal) regarding your money? Some of the best money moves a 50-year-old woman or man can make are reevaluating retirement savings goals, recalculating how to reach them and resetting how long it's going to take to get there. Money circumstances have changed for everyone. You're not alone.

Decide what retirement lifestyle you want and then plan accordingly. Be sure to continue setting money aside for retirement even if/when you've actually retired. We're all living longer these days (women on average five years longer than men) and will need money for a longer period of time than previous generations. Scale back on taking risks with your money (such as making personal loans that might not be paid back), crunch the numbers from all your income streams (Social Security, pension, etc.) to determine how to best allocate your assets, and "right-size" your housing costs (perhaps by refinancing, considering reverse mortgage or moving to a smaller home).

You can also adjust your money mentality to more easily cover your living expenses and lifestyle when you retire by saving more than 35 percent of your income for retirement, maxing out all tax-deferred retirement account options and "catch up" provision options, and contributing to either a traditional Individual Retirement Account (IRA) or a Roth IRA. And be sure you have all your retirement accounts in order – you want to make sure you don't leave money on the table and that your beneficiary choice isn't outdated.

When it comes to saving money, the best habit is to employ an autopilot system. Set up automatic deductions so that a certain amount of money from each paycheck goes directly into an online account. This is your "It's All About Me" money – money you control and commit to putting toward replenishing your personal nest egg. Consider this your new Money Pocket Change mind-set. Good expandable habits are asset forming!

Val-uable Money Tip:
Good expandable habits are asset forming!

Taking personal responsibility regarding your money and other assets will make our lives (and, after we die, our heirs' lives) less taxing. So get long-term-care insurance, revise or update your will, check beneficiary designations, resist the urge to loan money you can't afford to lose (including loans to family) and consider postponing retirement if you don't have enough saved.

If 40 is the new 30 and 60 the new 50, chances are boomers will have many productive years ahead. And while Ted Turner was born in the late 1930s, he can certainly be counted among the *unretired* group – by choice. His words, "You should set goals beyond your reach so you always have something to live for," make a lot of sense. As we get older, goals that include financial rewards provide us with purpose and, most important, security.

It's Your Money So Take It Personally

Chapter 10

—ɯɯ—

A Futurist View

*"For tomorrow belongs to the people who prepare
for it today." — African Proverb*

No matter your age, everyone must continually
focus their energies on developing a financial
blueprint that will meet day-to-day needs while
making money work for future needs – that is,
retirement.

Whether you're married, in a committed
relationship, suddenly single or single by choice, you
will need a trusted partner or partners in learning

(such as a financially astute friend or fellow members of an investment club) to help you aspire to see a bigger picture of your future than you might see for yourself.

My husband, Robert, is an emerging-markets strategist who provides advisory and consulting services that help businesses create sustainable, cost-effective diversity and inclusion practices.

We often present workshops and lectures together. As a couple, we tell young people that a good relationship is made up of two people who are both whole unto themselves, with their own careers and direction, and have the ability to collaborate through progressively honest, open communication.

Challenges Are Opportunities

Each generation has its challenges. For example, our generation saw the first transition of women to the workforce – a shift that impacted both men and women simultaneously. It was a difficult time and fractured many relationships, as long-standing gender-specific roles were challenged and reconfigured. Thankfully, many of the walls surrounding gender and race in the workplace have been knocked down. While pockets of discrimination exist, young people today – perhaps more than any other demographic – understand that collaboration (also known as co-creation), when combined with knowledge, is a powerful tool. Today's young workers tend to look at a person's skill set rather than a person's gender, color, religion or ethnicity.

Regardless whether it's with a spouse, partner, member of your money posse or your personal advisor, a teamwork approach to identifying, setting and reaching a goal requires cooperation and allows roles to be clearly defined. Ultimately, that will highlight each contributor's winning traits.

For example, Robert sees challenges as opportunities. When I think of him, both personally and professionally, I value that he approaches every situation with what I call his "40,000-foot view." He is like a pilot surveying the land below – the big picture and all its moving parts. He often says, "In order to push forward, you must understand your vision of the future."

In many ways, I am interpreter and translator for what I call "Robert speak." This is not because he doesn't speak eloquently and clearly; he does. Rather, he's thinking ahead to such a degree that oftentimes it takes people a little while to catch up to his thought processes. He's mentally speeding down the highway, and I'm providing directions for which exit (topic) to take. That's because he is already there, waiting and primed with an overview assessment of the situation or new circumstances. Understanding this aspect of his personality (the detailed business overview) lets mine (the detailed personal money focus) better manage and accommodate our lives.

As with many couples who work toward a common goal, we serve as a bridge for each other. With the bridge in place, our audiences seem quite comfortable discussing varying concepts that populate the financial and business worlds in which we all live. To alter an engrained approach to anything, especially money, requires a change of attitude and thinking. But doing that isn't as hard as you think.

Focus on this basic fact: You cannot exceed your available resources. Where you live, how you live, who you provide for, health concerns; these variables all add up to a dollar figure. Each of us must be responsible for making this assessment and measuring it against our individual financial means. To ignore and exceed this bottom-line metric – to make decisions that will put more demands on your ability to meet the needs of yourself, your family and your community – will impede our country's ability to successfully recover from this Great Recession. All matters of your life must be recalculated with money metrics in mind. It's not simply controlling money matters but all "matters" in your life.

Regarding this topic, I recently spoke with Bob McTeer, former president of the Federal Reserve Bank of Dallas and a fellow at the National Center for Policy Analysis, which covers macro-economic issues, including monetary policy, fiscal policy, tax policy and education policy.

"As we move beyond the financial turmoil and recession, we must remember that we can't count on policy-makers to protect us from their mistakes as well as those of our own making," says McTeer. "It's a matter of urgency that we take responsibility for the prosperity of ourselves as well as our children's generation. Economic education and financial literacy cannot be left to others. They are essential to our individual prosperity and our collective recovery."

Val-uable Money Tip:
You can't exceed your available resources.

This country no longer has just three generations living simultaneously. We now have at least four and, if great grandparents are in the picture, then potentially five. Many baby boomers created two generations. Robert and I have friends who are in their 60s, like us, and have children in their 30s as well as 6- and 7-year-old children from a subsequent relationship. As a consequence, many boomers are responsible for taking care of children in dramatically different age brackets – with costly current and future needs – in addition to their parents. This is a new dynamic.

Robert says, "The future is here *now,* but baby boomers — are trying to warm up and re-cook what we've known and trying to force feed it into our respective futures as a way to control power. Understanding the views and positions of younger generations, those of our children, can be instrumental in helping us boomers succeed."

Boomers represent the largest mass graying our country has ever seen. We're aware of how we contributed to the Great Recession. My husband says of our generation, "You know what you *paid* for something, but you didn't know what it would *cost* you. Our generation got caught up in this circumstance, and we slowly became owned by the things we bought. This was perhaps only truly realized when the Great Recession hit."

Continue to Pay It Forward

When I talk to young people about what has happened as a result of this recession, I focus the conversation on basic American economic concepts because often they are underappreciated.

I'm particularly enamored by both phrase and the concept of *"paying it forward."* The expression was popularized by Robert A. Heinlein in his book *Between Planets*, published in 1951. It is used to describe the idea of asking that a good deed be repaid by having it done for others instead of you. With respect to money, the expression specifically refers to a creditor that offers a debtor the option of "paying" the debt *forward* by lending the amount to a third person instead of paying the debt *back* by returning it to the creditor.

In many respects, when it comes to teaching economics and how money flows up and trickles down, the educational system has failed. There is no mandated standard by which our nation's schools prepare students to be financially literate before graduating. The results are clear; simply look at the amount of bad debt the average college graduate shoulders as they are handed their diploma. The only bright side to this issue is that we have but one direction to move from this gloomy financial picture: up!

"We do a poor job of teaching our kids about capitalism. If I had my way," says Robert, "it would be mandatory education from the first through the twelfth grade. We got into trouble as a nation because too many do not know how it works," he continued. "Capitalism isn't situational ethics. For too long we have based capitalism on circumstances as opposed to understanding that it's the science by which we built this country."

Traits of Wealthy People

Every American must understand that to build wealth you have to invest your time and money. If saving to invest and investing to build wealth is your goal – and it should be – let's take a look at how Abel Cheng's blog, Business Diary, describes the traits of wealthy people:

- **Persistence.** For anyone, on the way to achieving a goal, you will face obstacles, right? Wealth is achieved by negotiating one's way around or through numerous obstacles persistently.

- **Businesspeople or investors in businesses.** Think about it. The richest people we've heard about all own companies, and when asked they say that to create wealth, you must involve yourself in business because that's where the money is.

- **Innovative.** Innovation ensures you'll be among the ones who come up with new ideas and new ideas can create wealth. They tend to do what they absolutely love and love it so much that they forget they're actually working.

- **Leverage.** They know when to let go and they know not to try and do everything themselves.

From the above list, it appears that wealthy people embrace the philosophy that to whom much is given, much is expected. Therefore, they share the trait of giving back by supporting causes in which they believe. Because extremely wealthy people tend to believe that the greatest asset in the world is your mind, they value and participate in continuing education, which they understand can't always be given for free.

Grow Your Own

What will most impact the future is where jobs will be created and by whom. In the African American community, the phrase "grow your own" is common. It is based on the theory that the village (the neighborhood) supports and nurtures talent. It was and is a form of mentoring. It's the idea that those who *know* share information with those who *need* to know.

Mentoring is not a new idea, but there is an important difference in the 21st century approach. Mentoring is now a process by which those who *know* often are talking to people who *know more*. Conventional wisdom suggested that by the time we reached midlife, younger people would be voraciously accessing the crumbs of our acquired knowledge and life experiences. But our boomer generation is finding out that *our* mentors are often our grandchildren, our children and their friends, and that now is the time and this is the place where we're collectively learning to co-create. There's no stigma attached to being mentored by a 21-year-old when you're 40, 50 or 70. Information is being accessed and found in previously unlikely places.

Our generation grew up with a local economy in mind. Today, the younger workforce is accustomed to diverse races, cultures and backgrounds coming together for one purpose: commerce.

Learned $trategies

If the date October 27, 1997, doesn't ring a financial bell for you, it should. It was the day the Hong Kong stock market collapsed. The Hang Seng Index plummeted, causing massive selloffs in financial markets around the world and initiating a 554-point plunge in the Dow Jones Industrial

Average. It was the day automatic trading curbs – or collars, as they're also called – went into effect. The protocols of such curbs have now changed, but back then, they would halt trading for half an hour if the market fell 350 points or for an hour if it went down 550 points.

Those curbs had never been used before that day. As a result of the Hong Kong market's crash, the Dow shot past its first collar. Trading halted for 30 minutes. When trading resumed, so did the freefall – like a hot knife through butter, the Dow lost another 200 points. Down 550, with less than half an hour left to the closing bell, trading was halted for the day. The financial repercussions were felt around the world.

Working that story as a financial journalist absolutely solidified my commitment to positively impact people's financial futures. Not all investors had a plan in place to take advantage of "the sale"– the bargain-hunting, bottom-fishing opportunities that such an incident (the market meltdown) creates. This was a huge lost opportunity for many investors. Good companies were available at dramatically lower prices, but many would-be investors who tried to jump in and buy were too late. The lesson that should be remembered from 1997 is the same lesson today: In order to learn from market blunders, reassess, reorganize and realign your financial plan so that you have a strategy in place to be proactive rather than reactive when the market swings.

Everyone needs to employ a "what-to-do-if" financial fallback for just about every scenario. Not enough of us, however, have a clearly stated financial plan that allows us to take advantage of financial opportunities such as the massive selloff of October 27, 1997. And even after that missed opportunity, how many of us in the *14 years* since then have restructured our fiscal strategies to be beneficiaries rather than victims of market fluctuations and volatility? It is one thing to have lived and learned. It's quite another to live, learn, implement and succeed.

Deposits Into Your Emotional Bank Account

In the final analysis, having the conviction to change your life and the lives of those close to you whom you love and respect will go a long way in shaping who you are as a person – professionally, personally and for our purposes here, financially.

I believe in assets, both of the wallet and of the heart. I was the recipient of an extremely nurturing form of perfectionism that came from the loving hands of my 20-year-old mother, who married my father three weeks before her 17th birthday. When I was born, I became her real-life doll, and she took exemplary care of me. Everything she did for me and with me was as perfectly orchestrated as she could make it. Perfection had been an important and early discipline for this child bride to master. Though she was the teenage wife of a young Army-Air Force lieutenant who was just a few years her senior, she was a *military wife* now and in the midst of "older women already in their 30s!"

My mom became known for always being stylishly appropriate. It was one of her greatest assets, especially in the midst of military life. Whatever the setting or the culture, she had a fashionably unique consistency in the way she dressed. Where did she learn that? From my dad.

My parents married at a very young age, as so many young couples did in those days. Mom was right out of high school; she and my dad said their vows in front of a justice of the peace while he was home on a short leave. She was the youngest of three children, and she was encouraged by my grandmother Mudd to accept my dad's proposal, relocate to her new in-law's place and await his return at the -end of World War II. Mudd wanted my mom settled and out of a home that had been ruled by a harsh disciplinarian and was about to break apart.

A few weeks after they were married, my dad arrived home to change into his military dress uniform and pick up Mom for a formal squadron gathering with the base commander. He found her dressed like the 17-year-old that she was, in her best pleated skirt, white Angora sweater, matching socks and black Mary Jane shoes. Dad told her she looked beautiful, but that he'd like her to save that outfit to wear when just the two of them went out to dinner because in the Air Force there was a *uniform for wives.* "The *older* women usually wear a cocktail dress to events like tonight," he said. "Let's go get one for you!"

And so it was that every Friday of the early weeks of my mother's married life my dad would take her shopping for pieces of her "uniform." One Friday it was for hats. Another Friday it was for shoes. The next time was for suits, and yet another time for purses. My parents have been gone more than eight years now, but this story will always be special – the memory of how tenderly Bill brought Vicki into the world of *women of a certain age.*

It was this environment that taught me to recognize the value of different kinds of assets in our lives. Money is an asset and certainly matters. We should make deposits into our savings and retirement accounts on a regular and committed basis. But memories matter, too. They're priceless assets and should be considered valuable deposits into our emotional bank accounts.

The African proverb states, "For tomorrow belongs to the people who prepare for it today." It's with both emotional and financial preparation that a solid foundation is formed. No matter your age or generational tie, let *It's Your Money So Take It Personally*® be your guide to helping you build emotional and financial bridges for generations to come.

We're all unique and special in our own way. Our actions are best reflected in the reactions of those who surround and support us. As a "toucher," I would like to have the ability to reach out and connect with you so that you understand you're not alone as you reset the course of your financial future. I'm here for the entire journey, no matter the number of *mi$$ed-takes* you think you've made.

Framed in my office is a hand-painted poster that beautifully illustrates the progression of 12 roses opening from tiny green buds into a bright, full pink bloom. A quotation under the picture reads, "The day came when the risk to remain closed in a bud became more painful than the risk it took to blossom."

If you've read this far, I trust you will nurture your financial bouquet so that it blossoms and blooms with vibrancy and vitality. In doing so you will change how you manage your finances from a rearview mirror (tight bud) approach to a progressive, forward-looking (full bloom) approach. By resetting your money habits and moving toward self-reliance through financial emancipation, you will create your new normal regarding how you handle money. You'll know that rather than your money controlling you, you are controlling it.

Here's to you health and wealth! *It's your money so take it personally*®.

Chapter 11

Resources and Recommendations

"No finite point has meaning without an infinite reference point." — Jean-Paul Sartre

Together, as writer and reader, we've been on a journey, investigating and exploring the variables that influence financial behaviors. Let this final chapter be your reference point moving forward. Here you will find the necessary mental tools and various other resources to calculate and plan your financial future.

We began by discussing the B word, budget (or a spending plan). An excellent resource for setting a monthly and yearly budget can be found at Bankrate. com. This site offers free calculators for loans and computing credit card payoffs, interest rates for CDs and retirement savings, among others. Worksheets are provided to help create a family spending plan, emergency fund and monthly calendar, as well as track daily expenses and determine your net worth. For more information, visit: www.bankrate.com/calculators.aspx.

Additional online financial planning resources I recommend include:

- My website www.valeriecolemanmorris.com

- www.CNNMoney.com

- Kiplinger's Personal Finance magazine, at www.kiplinger.com

- www.feedthepig.org

Credit Report and Credit Score

The best way to be in control of your financial future is to know and *understand* what's being said about you and your money. As advice columnist Ann Landers said, "The naked truth is always better than the best dressed lie." That's why faithfully getting your free annual credit report online, by mail or by fax every year – and reading it – is mandatory.

Your credit report speaks volumes. It represents your discipline, or lack thereof, with money over time. Good credit adds up to a good credit score. Score big and you get the best interest rates, even in tough times.

You've likely heard commercials with catchy jingles telling you that getting your credit report at a certain website is free. Well, it is, but not without a catch. After all, you have to figure the commercials for these advertised services cost money. The credit report *is* free, but the fine print will likely result in monthly charges, unless you cancel your account. You are required to "opt out" within a short period of time or you'll pay a recurring monthly bill for membership in a credit-monitoring service. Anytime a credit-report site requires your credit card information in order for you to access your free annual report it should be a red flag. And as for getting your credit *score* from them, that requires payment.

Instead, visit www.annualcreditreport.com, a free, centralized, government-endorsed service created by the three nationwide consumer credit-reporting companies, Equifax, Experian and TransUnion, all of which are in compliance with the Fair and Accurate Credit Transactions Act (FACTA). To order your credit report by phone, call 1-877-322-8228.

In addition, I recommend the following websites: www.credit.com and www.quizzle.com.

Because you are eligible for one free report per year from each company, I suggest requesting one in January, one in July and the last in December. *It's your money so take it personally*® by welcoming and using this additional access to keep track of your money history. With this approach, you will have a handle on any and all activity relating to your credit report throughout the calendar year. And remember, the only time a credit check negatively impacts your credit report is when a creditor accesses it, not you. When you request your own credit report, it's considered a soft inquiry. Those inquiries are seen only by you, the consumer, and don't impact your credit score.

Starting From Scratch: How to Save a Million

If you want to retire with a million dollars, it's best to start early. But it's never too late to figure out how to catch up. Courtesy of *Kiplinger's Personal Finance* magazine's *Retirement Planning Guide,* the table that follows shows how much you need to save each month to accumulate $1 million by age 65, along with the strategies to achieve it. If your goal is lower or higher than a million dollars, go to www.kiplinger. com/links/whatyouneed to calculate how much you must save monthly.

HOW TO MAKE A MILLION Strategies for saving at every age

The table below shows how much you need to save each month to accumulate $1 million by age 65, along with strategies to fit retirement saving into the rest of your life. At age 25, you're starting from scratch. At ages 35, 45 and 55, we assume you already have money invested in a 401(k) or similar tax-deferred retirement account, on which you're earning 8% annually in a diversified portfolio. But keep in mind that even modest inflation of 3% will cut your buying power in half in 25 years, so you may need to save even more.

IF YOU'RE **25**	IF YOU'RE **35**	IF YOU'RE **45**	IF YOU'RE **55**
YOU'VE SAVED **$0**	YOU'VE SAVED **$0**	YOU'VE SAVED **$0**	YOU'VE SAVED **$0**
WHAT YOU NEED TO SAVE PER MONTH **$286**	WHAT YOU NEED TO SAVE PER MONTH **$671**	WHAT YOU NEED TO SAVE PER MONTH **$1,698**	WHAT YOU NEED TO SAVE PER MONTH **$5,466**
	YOU'VE SAVED **$50,000**	YOU'VE SAVED **$50,000**	YOU'VE SAVED **$50,000**
	WHAT YOU NEED TO SAVE PER MONTH **$304**	WHAT YOU NEED TO SAVE PER MONTH **$1,298**	WHAT YOU NEED TO SAVE PER MONTH **$4,859**
		YOU'VE SAVED **$100,000**	YOU'VE SAVED **$100,000**
		WHAT YOU NEED TO SAVE PER MONTH **$861**	WHAT YOU NEED TO SAVE PER MONTH **$4,253**
			YOU'VE SAVED **$200,000**
			WHAT YOU NEED TO SAVE PER MONTH **$3,040**

IF YOU'RE 25

YOU'RE JUST STARTING YOUR CAREER, SO THIS IS YOUR CHANCE TO BUILD A SOLID FINANCIAL FOUNDATION. TIME IS ON YOUR SIDE.

Contribute enough to your company 401(k) plan to **CAPTURE YOUR EMPLOYER MATCH.** If you don't have a retirement plan at work, fund an IRA.

You'll be investing for 30 years or more, so you can afford to **KEEP 100% OF YOUR ACCOUNT IN STOCKS.**

PAY DOWN CREDIT CARDS AND OTHER HIGH-INTEREST DEBT. That will free up money to save for a house.

SET UP AN EMERGENCY FUND equal to three to six months of take-home pay. Stash it in a readily accessible account in an online bank that pays higher interest than traditional banks.

$1 MILLION WILL BE WORTH $307,000 in 40 years.

IF YOU'RE 35

YOU MAY BE STARTING A FAMILY OR PREPARING TO BUY A HOME. BALANCE YOUR SHORT-TERM NEEDS WITH YOUR LONG-TERM SAVINGS GOALS.

AIM TO SAVE 15% OF YOUR GROSS INCOME (including an employer match) in your 401(k). If one parent leaves work to care for the kids, consider opening a spousal IRA.

Shift your assets to **90% STOCKS AND 10% BONDS.**

INVEST IN A 529 COLLEGE-SAVINGS PLAN. Many states offer a tax deduction for your contribution, and qualified distributions are exempt from federal taxes.

$1 MILLION WILL BE WORTH $412,000 in 30 years.

IF YOU'RE 45

YOU MAY BE JUGGLING THE NEEDS OF A GROWING FAMILY AND AGING PARENTS, BUT DON'T TAKE A BREAK FROM RETIREMENT SAVINGS.

You can **CONTRIBUTE UP TO $16,500 TO A 401(K)** or similar workplace-based retirement plan in 2010 or $5,000 to an IRA. Roll over retirement savings from previous jobs into an IRA.

Adjust your asset allocation to **80% STOCKS AND 20% BONDS.**

DON'T PUT YOUR KIDS' COLLEGE COSTS AHEAD OF RETIREMENT.

$1 MILLION WILL BE WORTH $554,000 in 20 years.

IF YOU'RE 55

TAKE ADVANTAGE OF YOUR PEAK EARNING YEARS TO ADD AN EXTRA $5,500 **IN CATCH-UP CONTRIBUTIONS** to your 401(k) savings and an extra $1,000 to your IRA.

As you near retirement, reallocate your portfolio to **70% STOCKS AND 30% BONDS.**

Estimate your retirement expenses and your projected income. If you're coming up short, **CONSIDER WORKING A FEW MORE YEARS.**

$1 MILLION WILL BE WORTH $744,000 in ten years.

IS YOUR RETIREMENT SAVING PLAN ON COURSE? | Go to kiplinger.com/tools/retirement-savings-calculator.html

Financial Recommendations for all Ages

Create a Secure Electronic File

Many people say that you should never write down all your financial information in one place for fear of it being compromised. I disagree. I recommend that you create a secure electronic file.

We are told to use different passwords, make them case-sensitive (or not), and use special characters mixed with numbers. Then you're supposed to remember them all. When you can't, you are prompted to reset passwords to access your accounts. That's why most people (despite admonitions) use familiar information they can remember, such as their birth date, address or wedding anniversary. And people typically use the same couple of passwords for everything. Creating a secure document allows you to have multiple combinations of various passwords that are written down for your reference. And I believe that you are fully capable of accepting responsibility for keeping this document secure.

Money in Your 20s:
- Priority one: Create a budget and set parameters on spending.

- Priority two: Pay down debt.

- Priority three: Repeat the money mantra, *save not spend.*

- Build an emergency fund with at least three to six months' worth of living expenses.

- Consider consolidating student loans.

- Consider purchasing prepaid spending cards – they force you to stay within the amount on the card.

- Limit credit card use.

- Pay more than the minimum due, on time, every month.

- Set realistic goals – they'll influence your saving and investing.

- Join your employer's savings plan as soon as you're eligible.

- Revise or update your will. Make one if you don't have one.

- Create a *secure* file that lists every detail of your financial footprint–account names, passwords, numbers, contact information, PINs, telephone code, etc. Give the file an abstract name you'll remember, print one copy and put it in a safe place for reference.

Money in Your 30s:

- Get serious about retirement savings.

- Catch up on other savings (your emergency fund, education savings and money for other long-term goals).

- Set new spending controls with each major life change (marriage, birth, death, divorce, layoff) that may set you back financially.

- If you are a business owner, establish a retirement plan – such as a traditional IRA, a SEP IRA or a solo 401(k) – in order to set aside tax-deductible, tax-deferred money.

- Start and maintain an emergency reserve fund (three to six months if you're an employee; 12 months if self-employed).

- Protect your assets. Term life insurance is a necessity for growing families.

- Set up and maintain adequate disability insurance.

- Consolidate and roll over retirement funds so that you have greater control over your money. Note that when you roll over money from one account to another you should never have the check made out in your name. If the company makes the check out to you, it is required to withhold 20 percent for taxes. To avoid the 20 percent withholding, you must arrange for a "direct" rollover of the funds in the name of your new account custodian.

- Purchase an apartment, condo or house.

- If married, be sure your spouse is on the same financial page. If planning to marry, talk openly before marriage about how you'll manage the money: separately, joint account, or combination of the two?

- Have a family spending plan. Be especially careful about overspending on the children.

- Don't put your child's college education before saving for your own retirement. You want to provide for your children, but not to the detriment of your own retirement future.

- Revise or update your will.

- Create a *secure* file that lists every detail of your financial footprint: account names, numbers, contact information, PINs, telephone code, etc.

Money in Your 40s:
- Eliminate debt.

- Reassess priorities to make room for saving for retirement.

- Build an emergency fund with three to six months' worth of living expenses.

- Maximize employer-sponsored pretax savings plans.

- Reevaluate and track investments closely.

- Adjust life insurance coverage because your needs and goals have likely changed.

- Open additional tax-sheltered investments – savings outside your employer-sponsored plan is always smart.

- Keep spending under control. You don't want to overextend yourself. Leave yourself financial breathing room.

- Prepare for the possibility of divorce or widowhood – both can be financially devastating. Revise or update your will.

- Create a *secure* file that lists every detail of your financial footprint: account names, passwords, numbers, contact information, PINs, telephone code, etc.

Money in Your 50s:
- The closer to retirement you get, the more you need to scale back on risky investments, firm up retirement options and keep track of assets.

- Decide what kind of retirement lifestyle you want and plan and save accordingly.

- With the assistance of a financial planning specialist, consider all of your income (from Social Security, pensions and elsewhere) to help determine how much risk is right for you as an investor at this stage of your life.

- Contribute to a traditional IRA or Roth IRA.

- Build an emergency fund with three to six months' worth of living expenses.

- "Right-size" housing costs. Consider moving from a large home to a smaller one.

- Unless independently financially secure, stop giving money to relatives/children.

- Adjust your life insurance. Make sure both husband and wife have adequate insurance to cover pre-retirement earning.

- Invest in long-term-care insurance. It's still affordable at this age.

- Take care of aging parents: deal with end-of-life issues and how you fit into their future, and what may be required of you emotionally and financially.

- Revise or update your will.

- Create a *secure* file that lists every detail of your financial footprint: account names, passwords, numbers, contact information, PINs, telephone code, etc.

Money in Your 60s:

- Save more than 35 percent of your income for retirement.

- Consider postponing retirement if you don't have enough saved.

- Contribute to a traditional IRA or Roth IRA.

- Max out all tax-deferred retirement account options and "catch up" provision options.

- Get long-term-care insurance.

- Revise or update your will.

- Check beneficiary designations on all important documents.

- Resist the urge to loan money you can't afford to lose, including loans to family.

- Create a *secure* file that lists every detail of your financial footprint: account names, passwords, numbers, contact information, PINs, telephone code, etc.

Money in Your 70s and Beyond:

- Be tax smart with your retirement savings. With the assistance of a certified financial specialist, figure out which accounts to access and in what order.

- Leave tax-deferred accounts untouched as long as possible to take advantage of tax-free compounding. (Exception: At age 70½ be sure to take the minimum required withdrawals from them or you'll pay hefty IRS penalties.)

- Working with a trusted, certified financial specialist, invest in a diversified portfolio of stock and bond funds to improve the odds you won't outlive your money.

- Be sure to ask your trusted advisor if an income annuity is right for you. An annuity ensures you keep a stream of income even if other assets run dry. That guaranteed income will reduce the amount you take from savings and serve as a buffer against damage to your investment portfolio during market downturns.

- Revise or update your will.

- Create a *secure* file that lists every detail of your financial footprint: account names, passwords, numbers, contact information, PINs, telephone code, etc.

Your Financial Calendar

Finally, I would like to leave you with a financial calendar to-do list. These are some financial fundamentals that we all need to address every year. With this tool, you will have a handle on your money, not the other way around. You can read this book all at once or pick it up for monthly suggestions and apply them to your situation accordingly. The idea is to have at least a standing, monthly date with your money to continue learning more about what it can do for you.

These are doable, incremental, achievable money-management goals that will alleviate a lot of your money anxieties. Your mind-set for this money-management exercise need only be: *once a month is all it takes.*

January: Get one of your free annual credit reports.
- Only from www.annualcreditreport.com.

- Credit reports show how you handle debt, how much you owe and how you pay your bills.

- Read them, challenge in writing anything that's incorrect or not yours.

- It's important that you know what's being said about you and your money.

February: Organize your documents in preparation for doing your taxes.

- Use folders and label them (receipts, insurance, investments, etc.).

- Create a safe place to store the documents.

- Buy a shredder – preferably confetti-cut, but any shredder is better than tossing whole documents into the recycling.

- Shred old documents (more than seven years) or documents you no longer need–anything that has your name and personal information.

March: Review all of your insurance policies.

- Review life, health, disability, long-term care, property, auto and casualty insurance.

- Confirm what type of life insurance policy you have (term, whole, universal or variable).

- Money Central has an online calculator to help you figure out how much insurance you need: http://money.msn.com/life-insurance/life-insurance-quotes.aspx

- Know your policy number. It's essential for any claim or customer-service need.

- Know the date the policy was issued.

April: *Review debt and tax strategies.*

- Review credit card debt as well as mortgages, auto loans and any other long-term obligations.

- Check to see whether rates and/or terms have changed.

- Begin planning how to reduce -next year's income taxes.

- If you got a tax *refund,* adjust your withholding to increase your take home pay.

May: *Review your will and update it (65 percent of Americans do not have a will).*

- Reviewing your will is especially important if you've had major life changes, such as births, deaths, a divorce, a marriage, a job loss or a relocation.

- A will helps you exercise your rights and have your wishes respected.

- In the absence of a will, spouses and/or domestic partners have very few rights and can be left with very little.

- Dying without a will means dear friends, your favorite charity or church will be shut out from inheriting anything from you.

- A simple will is the only way you can

control what happens with your affairs and possessions after you're gone.

- Note: If you have children and no will, the state will decide their guardianship if both parents are deceased.

June: *Find a certified financial planner.*
- Check with the National Association of Personal Financial Advisors (at http://www.napfa.org), whose members provide strictly fee-only services.

- Look for advisors with at least five years of experience, and check their background.

- Ask about the kind of client and financial situations with which they like to work.

- Be sure to know how they get paid (hourly, by the job or as a percentage of the assets they manage).

July: *Review employer-matched savings programs.*
- Attend your company's "Open Enrollment" meetings.

- The literature may be dense, but read it thoroughly as it applies to you and your family's needs.

- Many companies have dramatically changed rules, contribution levels and qualifications.

- Confirm that programs in which you're enrolled or interested are still available.

- Make sure you're contributing at the level necessary to qualify for your employer's match.

- Check the diversity of your investment portfolio.

August: Determine your net worth.
- List the value of all your assets and possessions.

- List your liabilities and debt.

- This exercise helps accurately determine the level of home/renters insurance you need.

- Have memorabilia, collections or beloved heirlooms appraised and certified.

September: Go paperless with bills.
- Convert to online banking and bill paying.

- Every account that's paperless can be retrieved online 24 hours a day.

- Saves time and money – no stamps needed.

October: *Create an automatic savings contribution.*

- Most people save as an afterthought. That's thinking backward.

- The easiest money to save is money you never see.

- Set up direct deposits from your paycheck, which provides automatic, recurring transfers to move money from checking to savings as appropriate.

- If no direct deposit is available, link checking and savings together and establish automated transfers between accounts at regular intervals.

November: *Check your retirement contribution.*

- Set up the contribution to coincide with your pay day.

- The best time to start saving for your retirement is in your 20s, when you have time on your side. Your money can grow significantly because it earns interest on top of interest.

- Know how much money you need to save for retirement (use online calculators from one of the two financial resources listed earlier).

December: *Analyze your auto insurance coverage.*

- Seek good advice from a credentialed, experienced professional, such as your insurance broker or certified financial planner.

- Shop around among brand names and independents.

- Make sure you're getting the best deal and are adequately covered.

- Depending on your assets, consider an umbrella policy – it covers your home and automobile.

Move Forward With Confidence

As Jean-Paul Sartre said, "No finite point has meaning without an infinite reference point." It is my hope and intention that you reference this chapter on a monthly basis, as it is a catchall of the information contained within *It's Your Money So Take It Personally*®.

Thanks for taking this journey with me. Here's to your health and wealth!

Afterword

David J. Teece

Professor of (Global) Business, Haas School of Business, University of California, Berkeley

The panoply of experiences and events that shaped Valerie Coleman Morris's character, values and personal finances are very evident in It's Your Money So Take It Personally®. In this book, one of CNN's most loved and respected former business anchors brings to common folks a deep and emotionally intellectual understanding of individual financial responsibility from cradle to grave. Valerie softly preaches financial prudence, while providing tools and tricks to make the task easier. She reminds us – in case we have already forgotten – that one shouldn't drift far into financial distress and impose burdens on family, friends and society. Rather, taking control of one's own finances and acting knowledgeably and prudently will bring a better life and a more pleasant retirement.

It's Your Money So Take It Personally® isn't just a tale about how the Great Recession has changed everything. It's a tale about how financial prudence over a lifetime, through good times and bad, will protect individuals and families.

Valerie gently puts across her message. She could talk about American financial irresponsibility – personal, corporate and governmental. She could jolt the reader with statistics about personal savings rates in China being more than ten times the savings rates in the U.S., or she could remind the reader that Australia and Chile have compulsory savings plans by law. Her style is not to castigate the reader for irresponsible and profligate consumption. Rather, her style is to nudge us toward taking financial responsibility, developing savings habits while young and postponing purchases until we can afford them. She encourages us to be prepared for the various stages of life: marriage, children, job relocations, divorce and even death. Hers is a personal story – some of which I am familiar with. It's a compelling and well-researched guide to personal financial responsibility. It's not a treatise on money management as such. One must first accumulate some savings before getting too deep into investment, and it's the former which is the focus of the book.

Valerie's aphorism will be enough for some. For most, the book will inform and energize readers to begin saving at an early age, to teach their children and grandchildren to do so, and to always think of their futures and the futures of others around them – family, friends and beyond. Turning a deaf ear to Valerie's underlying message is rendered impossible by close-to-home personal stories and heartfelt advice delivered in plain English by one of America's best financial commentators.

But changing bad habits isn't easy. Knowledge of consequences helps. Choosing peers who have better habits and who are supportive emotionally can assist mightily. Creating a budget and adhering to it, as Valerie advises, is a very big step, but it is only the first step. However, it will begin the process of putting one on the road to financial independence. Employers also respect financial prudence, and it will help one get a job and advance on the job. Virtuous circles can replace vicious circles.

Success in saving will open opportunities for purchasing a home and for other forms of investment. Prudent investment may not be as challenging; but it is not straightforward either. The best investment is probably in paying off credit card debt; the next, paying down the home mortgage. Thereafter, opportunities exist to benefit from investing in business enterprises (equity and debt) and in real estate. The required skills here are different, and investment strategies depend on stages of life, family situations and investment opportunities. Our vigorous and open capitalist economic system allows all to participate. Prudent investing benefits both the investor and the investee. An economy that has investment is an economy that will grow and generate jobs. Individual financial prudence begets societal and governmental prudence. Unfortunately, the reverse is also true, as we have been witnessing for quite some time now.

So putting mind over money matters not just for the individual. It matters for families, communities and for our nation. The age of mindless personal and public expenditures must end, and end quickly.